In his new album-book Only the Lover Sings, Matthew Clark has assembled voices, tough and tender, laser-focused at a horizon of hope. Clark's ability to draw out the passion of others, achieves for him a fresh vision where healing and joy can be known after loss and pain and failure. Take up and read. Open and listen... Come and see. You may find your own dark ladder downward leading you out onto a surprising open plain of possibility and light.

—Bruce Herman, painter

These essays and the songs they celebrate are altogether lovely, each one adding a new dimension of insight, purpose, comfort, and hope. The collection shines with variations on a theme, and the whole is so much greater than the sum of its parts. Matthew Clark joins the ranks of George Macdonald, G. K. Chesterton, C. S. Lewis, and others who connect head with heart, reason with imagination, and scripture with hard-won experience. The result is both a feast and a fellowship. I love it.

—Diana Pavlac Glyer, author of *Clay in the Potter's Hands,*
The Company They Keep, and *Bandersnatch: C. S. Lewis,*
J. R. R. Tolkien, and the Creative Collaboration of the Inklings.

If you've ever found yourself held back in life by your own doubt, fear, or shame, you know there are three kinds of friends—and three kinds of books—that can help you. One reaches in and pulls you out. The other just sits by your side and understands. 'Only the Lover Sings' is the rarest: it sits with you, and shares the kind of lived hope you can't shrug off.

—Brian Brown
Executive Director, The Anselm Society

Every once in a while, a sum is greater than its individual parts, and Matthew Clark has managed to bring about such a marvel while creating *Only the Lover Sings*. Matthew's work has long been tender, unique, vulnerable, and heartening. But in this latest project, he's collaborated with writers who thoughtfully interact with each main theme Matthew introduces. The resulting work is prismatic and harmonious, the fruit of faith in community. In these lonely, fragmented times, it's hopeful and healing to encounter their chorus of gentle and honest reflection. I think you're going to love Matthew's record. I think you're also going to love what a group of friends has grown from his roots.

—Rebecca Reynolds, author of *Courage, Dear Heart: Letters to a Weary World*

As a teenager and young adult, I filled many happy hours reading liner notes, copying lyrics into my journal, and exploring the credits of my favorite records. Streaming music online is robbing a generation of these delightful, tangible experiences. This is just one of the many reasons I have been so taken by Matthew Clark's *Only the Lover Sings*. In this album-book combo, Clark has coupled thoughtful meditations with songs that are a balm to my heart. This project is biblically rich, poetic, and honest. And, I am so glad I can find myself once again copying down lyrics into my journal!

—Leslie Bustard, co-founder of Square Halo Books, writer, poet, and editor of *Wild Things and Castles in the Sky: A Guide to Choosing the Best Books for Children*

Once at a youth camp, I was taught that every person alive bears 'ultimate' questions about meaning and origin. But, I believe, deeper than even those must be this single aching question: 'Am I loved?' There are many reasons, in a world pocked by cruelty and tragedy, that the answer to that question can be profoundly difficult to find. In this beautiful book of song and Scripture, essay and story, Matthew Clark helps his readers to the healing, redemptive, life-forming answer to that burning question by showing us that with God, 'belovedness is our starting point'. This is a gentle, redemptive work, a generous opening of Matthew's heart and a joyous response by fellow writers to his words, leading the reader ever deeper into the knowledge of God's real love; personal, present, invading our darkness and healing our souls.

—Sarah Clarkson, author of *This Beautiful Truth: How God's Goodness Breaks into Our Darkness*

ONLY THE LOVER SINGS

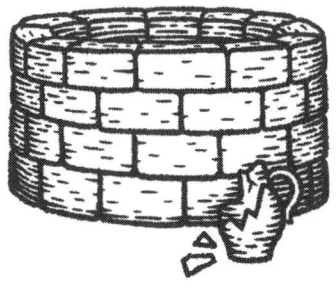

Part One of *The Well Trilogy*

Meditations on the Woman at the Well
· in STORY and SONG ·

Matthew Clark

© 2022 Matthew Clark

Published by Panim Press
132 W. Bradford Place, Madison, MS 39110

All songs written by Matthew Clark and published by Path in the Pines Music (ASCAP)
All rights reserved. No part of this book may be reproduced without permission from the publisher, except by a reviewer who may quote brief passages in a review; nor may any part of this book be reproduced, stored in a retrieval system or transmitted in any form by any means (electronic, mechanical, photocopying, recorded, or other), without permission from the publisher.

979-8-9856522-0-8 (*Only the Lover Sings* - paperback)
979-8-9856522-1-5 (*Only the Lover Sings* - hardcover)
979-8-9856522-2-2 (*Only the Lover Sings* - ebook)

All Scripture quotations, unless otherwise indicated, are taken from the Holy Bible, New International Version®, NIV®. Copyright ©1973, 1978, 1984, 2011 by Biblica, Inc.™ Used by permission of Zondervan. All rights reserved worldwide. www.zondervan.com The "NIV" and "New International Version" are trademarks registered in the United States Patent and Trademark Office by Biblica, Inc.™

Scripture quotations marked CSB have been taken from the Christian Standard Bible®, copyright © 2017 by Holman Bible Publishers. Used by permission. Christian Standard Bible® and CSB® are federally registered trademarks of Holman Bible Publishers.

Scripture quotations marked (ESV) are from the *ESV® Bible* (*The Holy Bible, English Standard Version®*), Copyright © 2001 by Crossway, a publishing ministry of Good News Publishers. Used by permission. All rights reserved.

Scripture quotations marked MSG are taken from THE MESSAGE, copyright © 1993, 2002, 2018 by Eugene H. Peterson. Used by permission of NavPress, represented by Tyndale House Publishers. All rights reserved.

Scripture quoted by permission. Quotations designated (NET) are from the NET Bible® copyright ©1996, 2019 by Biblical Studies Press, L.L.C. http://netbible.com All rights reserved.

Printed in the United States of America

ONLY THE LOVER SINGS

Part One of *The Well Trilogy*

by Matthew Clark

Andrew Roycroft
Lanier Ivester
Théa Rosenburg
Adam Whipple
Heidi White
Jessie Todd
Adam R. Nettesheim
Amy Baik Lee
Junius Johnson
Rex Bradshaw

Edited by Elisabeth Adams

For those who thirst.

My heart says of you, "Seek his face!"
Your face, LORD, I will seek.

Ps 27:8

Contents

Welcome 15

Introduction 19

1. Looking for You
   Andrew Roycroft - *A Stranger on the Road* 33

2. Every Beauty
   Lanier Ivester - *Eggardon Hill* 45

3. The Well
   Théa Rosenburg - *Below the Tideline* 57

4. Everything but You
   Adam Whipple - *In the Darkness of Noontide* 67

5. Trying to Get My Heart Back
   Heidi White - *Embracing a New Name: St. Photini* 77

6. The Heart of Our God
   Matthew Clark - *The Way Home* 87

7. Only the Lover Sings
   Jessie Todd - *Excavation* 101

8. The Return of the Prodigal Son
   Adam R. Nettesheim - *Learning to Walk Again* 111

9. I See a Light
   Amy Baik Lee - *The Sound of Eucatastrophe* 123

10. That Won't Stop Him
    Junius Johnson - *All You Have to Do Is Die: The Power of Abiding in Death* 133

11. Meet Me at the Well
    Rex Bradshaw - *The Digger's Tale* 142

Epilogue: *Gentleness Towards Each Face* 151

Acknowledgments 167

Contributors 171

Album Credits 177

Welcome

In your hands you hold the first in a trilogy of books. Or are these albums? What's going on here? Let me explain.

Back in August 2019, I dumped about fifty little recordings onto my phone. Some were partly finished songs, others were scraps of melodies, lyrical impressions, or things I'd hummed into my phone while half awake in the middle of the night. A few were second or third drafts of songs I liked, and a handful were over a decade old—songs I'd kept coming back to for some reason, rewritten over and over again, and wondered if I'd ever finish. The rest of that autumn, I drove around and listened to these recordings. I didn't have a project in mind. No big idea. But the more I listened, the more the songs seemed to group themselves like folks at a party finding their way to this or that conversation in a corner of the room.

Three distinct conversations surfaced. The first group of songs were talking about personal encounter, others about holding on in suffering, and still others were saying something about joy and coming home to the Lord. Life is noisy, and I felt like I was only catching snippets of these conversations, but from what I could hear, they were all connected. The songs may have gravitated to their own nooks in the room, but they were in the same room; they were having particular conversations within an overarching conversation. I was surprised to discover three albums taking shape.

Now, sometimes an idea shows up, and it gets no traction; I forget about it. But by the following spring, I was even more excited. I couldn't stop thinking about it. The only problem was that the songs needed a whole lot of attention, and they were only half the songs I would need to fill out the trilogy. As I prayed, I realized I'd need to take a deep dive into songwriting to pull this off. Ideally, I'd need a two- or three-month dedicated songwriting retreat. I couldn't see how that was going to happen.

Then, in March 2020, the pandemic lockdowns hit. I knew I wouldn't be able to tour that coming fall, so now that whole season was wide open. I sent an email to some friends in Colorado asking for advice and any leads on a place to retreat during the autumn months to work on this project. A three-month writing retreat? I was shooting for the moon. And the moon is what I got. Well, more specifically, *the* Moons.

Steve and Terri Moon were friends I'd met through The Anselm Society and The Cultivating Project. To my astonishment, they offered their guest room. Obviously they didn't understand; I would need to live there for a few months. Well, they *did* understand; I could stay as long as I liked. Their welcome and care was a direct provision from the Lord.

That retreat was beautiful, not to mention fruitful. Steve and Terri's generosity freed me to write all day, every day for over two months. Sixteen of the trilogy's thirty-three initial songs got major make-overs, and seventeen brand new songs showed up. That's the power of arts patronage. And the Moons were not the only patrons. A few years before, I'd begun raising support through my Patron Partners program, and this work would not be possible without the prayers and gifts of those friends as well.

But what about this book/album/essay collection thingy? Right. That.

Well, one thing the Lord has been hammering into my mind in the last few years is that bodies with only one part are no bodies at all; you can't be a person without other people. If that's true, then how could I expect to make an album in keeping with the relational shape of reality all by myself? Here was a chance to explore collaboration more deeply. Besides that, I'd gotten tired of my own voice. I wanted to be surprised, and it's hard to surprise yourself.

What if I invited writers I admired to join the conversation? What if I asked them not to review the songs, or analyze the songs, or critique the songs, but to *respond* to them? To lovingly cooperate with them? What if we all entered into the story together and collaborated in making it available through the various voices of music, lyric, and essay? And what if each album had a book? What if each album *was* both an album *and* a book? A balbum? An albook?

It would be a bit of an experiment, to be sure.

Now you're caught up on the short history of what I'm calling *The Well Trilogy*. I'll release an album and book each year for the next three years, until the trilogy is complete. (Then I will take a long nap.) Here's a quick overview of the core idea of each album:

Only the Lover Sings: Album One gets its narrative shape from the Samaritan woman's meeting with Jesus by a well. What failures and griefs obstruct our view of that face that smiles upon us and calls us his Beloved? What changes when our thirst is slaked as we finally see him seeing us?

A Tale of Two Trees: Album Two is about the fight to hold onto the light of that face as darkness closes in on us. Wasn't meeting Jesus supposed to fix everything? How do we endure *this*?

Can our parched throats still sing the songs of home, as home begins to feel like an empty promise? What decisions will we make when it seems like the well has run dry?

Where the River Goes: Album Three looks towards that blessed vision when every veil that clouds our sight is removed. We will meet Jesus face to face, evil and death will be no more, he will wipe away every tear, and Ezekiel's prophecy will come true: the well becomes a river, and everything will live where the river goes.

The only thing missing at this point is you. You are invited into this conversation, too. Come sit beside Jacob's well. Let's go looking together for this God who first came looking for us. Scary as it may seem to meet his gaze, *only the one who dares to look him full-on in the face finds out the shocking good news.*

Introduction

A Long Season of Grief

Beginning about seven years ago, I entered into a long season of grief and healing after divorce. It was traumatic, to say the least, and would have been even more so, had it not been for a little ragtag church plant that met in a borrowed gymnasium, and a few friends who held onto me. But the divorce was more than just a surprising twist in my own story, it was the brutal shredding of the book I had been reading. Much of how I had come to understand my life, myself, and my God would have to be rewritten now, because I could not have imagined the terrifying thing my life had become. Moments of despair had made their appearances on the pages before, of course, but during this season I found that I had no language or categories for the species of death that seemed to soak through every page of my life like an exploded bottle of India ink. My own story had become unrecognizable to me. Who was I now? I must admit I often dreamt of simply burning the tattered remains of my book, because I couldn't envision anything good to come. I felt my face was pressed up against an immovable "wall of black."[1]

---

[1] Matthew Clark, "You're Gonna Be Okay," Come Tell Your Story, Path in the Pines Music (ASCAP), 2014, Track 10.

One of the strange saving graces of the whole ordeal was its public nature. Because the thing was unhideable, I wasn't able to isolate myself in my grief as easily as I might have otherwise. Nor could I live in denial. Because people knew, there was no point in trying to convince anyone who checked on me that I was fine. I simply had to face the fact that there was no "going around" this thing; if I was to survive, I would have to go through it.

Before the divorce, I had been a worship leader for about ten years. Being in ministry, maybe I had begun to depend on a false sense of my own goodness. More likely I'd always been that way. The divorce was a failure that sprung the trap door of self esteem I'd been standing on. While talking with my (amazing) counselor Vicki about that sense of lost identity, I mentioned that I'd always wanted to be "good," to which she raised her eyebrows and uttered a long "ahhhh" before descending pen-in-hand upon her little notebook to record an apparently significant insight. We really do need a sense of goodness, if we're to feel that our presence in this world is justified, but most of the time we try to drum up what can only be received as a gift. It was painful to discover that much of my sense of goodness had been my own construction, but learning to receive my sense of belovedness as a gift from the Lord has turned out to be a relief.

So why do I bring all that up? I can assure you that it's not because I love to talk about it. But at this point I am just entering the strange territory of actually being thankful for the most painful thing that has ever happened to me. Don't worry, I'm not suggesting that God causes these kinds of things for our good. God didn't cause my marriage, the circumstances that led to its death, or the divorce. I wish I could blame him, but the only thing he's "guilty" of is beating me to rock bottom, where I was surprised to discover Jesus already bringing the light of his face to bear in the places where I had supposed even God wasn't allowed to go.

No, I bring it up because, like my friend Brian once pointed out, our griefs can become like knots along the previously smooth rope of our souls—knots that provide handholds for others sinking in the water as we let down the rope to them from our canoes.[2] I've found that to be true; my grief seemed to summon companions in suffering who tossed well-knotted ropes to me as I flailed in the 'whelming flood. What friends, artists, or authors have done that for you? During those first two years, Henri Nouwen was one such author whose little book *The Inner Voice of Love*[3] companioned me. He threw out his knotted rope and I clung to it. I have no idea who gave that little book to me or how many times I read it. I just *looped* it: whenever I finished, I turned to page one and started again.

In the same way, I hope that sharing my own experience can serve others. Granted, I won't pretend to know how, but I'm thinking it's worth the risk of tossing the rope out, if it helps someone discover they're not as alone as they had thought. At the very least, it should help make some sense of this album (and the trilogy it begins) by giving you some context for the songs. This project is emerging after long incubation in that extended season of grief that (oddly enough to me) held at its heart a healing encounter with Jesus. And these songs are a kind of record (no pun intended) of my own journey of despair visited by the surprise of God's unshakable lovingkindness. As an album, *Only the Lover Sings* bears witness to the reality of how desperately dried up the wells on which we've depended can get, and yet, how our most devastating thirst is evidence that our true destiny has always been to bathe forever in the Wellspring of Living Water. We are made for the love of God in Jesus.

"But," you may be asking, "why is this album called 'Only the Lover Sings'?" Well, (pun intended) I'm glad you asked.

---

[2] Clark, "Now There's Laughter," *Come Tell Your Story*, Track 9.
[3] Henri J. M. Nouwen, *The Inner Voice of Love: A Journey through Anguish to Freedom* (London: Darton Longman & Todd, 2014).

The Woman at the Well

Maybe you've experienced this too? The same conversation randomly comes up with multiple unconnected people over a few weeks? You start to notice a pattern of uncanny coincidences, and the breadcrumbs seem to be leading you somewhere. Like a plot thickening.

The Lord knows how each of us learns best, and this is one of the ways he gets my attention: some story, phrase, word, or conversation seems to pop up all over the place during a season. It usually takes a while for me to get the idea, but eventually I start to look closer.

During the years since my divorce, there has been a specific story that just keeps coming up again and again. I didn't go looking for it; I began to feel like it had come looking for me. That story was Jesus and the Samaritan woman at the well from John 4.

This is the scene that, over the last seven years, has become a kind of low-ground gathering place for the many rivulets of those uncanny coincidences I mentioned. The Lord kept dropping breadcrumbs, and the more I followed the pattern, the more I would wind up again and again in John 4, watching this woman meet this man. During this season, I found myself repeatedly invited to allow the encounter at Jacob's Well to give shape to my own life.

Henri Nouwen had a similar experience with the story of the prodigal son, and specifically Rembrandt's famous painting of the father tenderly receiving his lost child. Nouwen found that God's ministering presence pooled in the depiction of that story, cleansing and quenching him during a season of deadly thirst. Likewise, this particular encounter between Jesus and the Samaritan woman has since captivated my imagination, until seemingly impossible hope began to spring up within me, transforming those places of deep, withering despair.

You would be correct in thinking that after such a heartbreaking experience with marriage, marriage would be the last thing I'd want to think about. But, God, in his great wisdom and kindness, took my experience of broken human love and affirmed that very thirst as bearing witness to the supernatural love of Christ, because the story of this whole world is the story of a Groom proposing to a Bride. A Bride who for the most part has refused his proposal. But Jesus is a most devoted lover, to say the least, pursuing his Beloved all the way to hell and back. John 4 is a story about just how terrifying life can become when love goes wrong, and how surprisingly beautiful it can yet be when we come face to face with Jesus, the lover of our souls.

Needless to say, the Samaritan woman's story has made a lot of sense to me. These last several years, I have felt something like a shared understanding of bewilderment and loss, as she has walked with me through my own dark forest of grief. Take a few moments to imagine this woman with me:

She's *already* had five husbands; she's working on number six. Right down to the roots of our very essence we are relational creatures, so we understand ourselves by how we are received by others, who mirror us back to ourselves. The most basic example is a smile, signifying that someone is glad to be in our presence. But perhaps this woman is used to seeing herself dirty in the frowning muddy mirrors of the faces around her? Because we are made in the image of the Trinity, a communion of three persons, life loses all context and narrative when we are pulled like a single thread from the tapestry of loving community. That strand becomes *stranded*, and she is stranded from a healthy social fabric. Or, much like some animals do, humans call out to one another in a sort of echo-location that says, "Is anybody there? Am I really alone?" And we wait for a kind voice to return, "I am here with you." But she's called out to locate herself, and the voices that should echo back are either cold in their silence or cruel. She's lonely and lost, which is another way of saying *thirsty*. Very thirsty. She's dried up five wells already.

Now, nobody starts out thinking, "How can I make my life as miserable as possible?" In the beginning, at least, she wasn't some wicked floozy traipsing around town luring hapless men to her bower. Most likely she began just as young, naive, and hopeful for a life of love and happiness as the rest of us. Because only men could initiate divorces at the time, this woman was likely cast off by a string of husbands. Who knows why? Maybe she had some kind of defect, possibly infertility. But life's tragedies snowballed, and things got worse and worse. By the time you get to spouse number six, who among us wouldn't have ditched the virtuous life and filled the emptiness with any number of cynicism's many protective devices? Anybody would have resorted to street-smarts, having learned the hard way that the vulnerability goodness requires is much too costly in a world so cruel.

But today, she goes to a well and finds another man. A man who gently calls out to her from his own place of weariness and vulnerability, locating her in conversation with himself. Jesus goes first, pioneering a conversation by sharing his own thirst for connection. God-in-the-flesh calls out as if to say, "Is anyone there? Am I really alone?" And the Samaritan woman is a little shocked to be invited into his presence. He goes on to touch all the ragged strands of her threadbare life; he is interweaving himself with her shame. She is a bruised reed he will not break—a lonely one he intends to set in a family. Finally, as the encounter gets more and more uncomfortable, she wriggles and squirms to keep from having to face this man. She picks up her jar to leave. But just then something amazing happens—she turns to face him. At the last second, she sees him seeing her, and she suddenly sees herself in a previously unimaginable way: she is his Beloved.

Now, imagine: every well holds a little round mirror deep

underground at its center. Can you see it in your mind's eye? She had gazed into six muddy mirrors only to find herself trapped in a deep, dark place, unable to face herself with any hope. But by the end of her conversation with Jesus, the very Well from which Jacob's promise was drawn, she sees herself reflected in his tender and compelling gaze. Astonishingly, he is glad to be in her presence; there is an unexpected light in his face, and it dawns on her that he is mirroring back to her a glimmer of growing hope.

What exactly did she see that day on the face of our tired, thirsty Lord? Because, God knows, all of us long all our lives to see it ourselves, searching for it in every face we meet. Notably, we're not given a description of what the woman at the well sees. We're only allowed to see what happens as a result of what she saw. So, what is the result of coming face to face with Jesus? She blooms like a virgin bud facing a gladdening light—a burgeoning flower lifting its face towards the summons of gentle dawn. She sees Jesus seeing her, and in his face, she sees herself truly as God's Bride, radiant. Once she has seen him seeing her, she will only ever see herself as situated beneath the banner of the Lord's loving gaze.

And this is too good not to mention: My friend Esther pointed out that in the Bible, typically, when you see a man and woman meet at a well, guess what happens next? Somebody's getting married. It's a pattern in Scripture. As this bizarre meeting of Jesus and the Samaritan woman was retold, every Jewish reader would've picked up on the familiar plotline. So think about it. This woman has been through *five* husbands, is working on number *six*, and then she runs into a man at a well. And he's number . . . what? *Seven*. Jesus is himself the Sabbath; he's her seventh and final, her Sabbath husband. This poor worn-out woman can finally rest.

But this story is about so much more than just one woman's healing encounter. The One through whom creation was brought into being is putting the whole disordered cosmos back in order by replacing its discarded Sabbath Capstone. Buechner beautifully said that "the story of any one of us is in some measure the story of us all,"[4] and this story is like that. As much as it is about this one particular woman, it is about all of us, who are so worn out trying to live without our Sabbath Lord. As St. Augustine said, "Thou hast made us for thyself, O Lord, and our heart is restless until it finds its rest in thee." For a man with Augustine's past, I doubt those were just pretty words.

So, if the Sabbath himself has come to spread his banner of love over humanity, his Bride, then you and I are being asked, in the midst of our most dried-out, exhausted places, to look up and be surprised to find, not one more frowning mirror, but a face (oddly enough) delighting in us. Which leads me to this:

I want to see what she saw.

Beholding Jesus: A New Song

I'd like to tell you about a turning point towards the end of the first two years after my divorce. Those years were very dark, and nearly all my time was spent in constant anxiety, turmoil, and depression. One day, having worn myself out by spinning my wheels in the muddy rut of my fears and hopelessness, I looked up and across the room. In my mind's eye, I saw Jesus sitting on the gray bricks of the hearth like the rim of a well, calmly saying, "I'm still here, and when you're finished, I'll still be here."

My worst sins and rantings couldn't shake him. Jesus is so quietly constant in his love, and you can't intimidate him with your failure. I thought maybe he'd have changed his mind after all this mess, but his steady lovingkindness gave me the courage to keep going. Could there be new chapters in my book?

That Jesus had not budged was a surprising realization. He clearly cared deeply about me in the chaos I was experiencing, but

---
[4] Frederick Buechner, *The Sacred Journey* (San Francisco: HarperSanFrancisco, 1982).

though my whole world had changed, nothing had changed in the least for him. He counted the cost of choosing to commit himself to humanity long ago. While I was flipping out, he was patient, waiting for me to realize he loved me exactly the same as he always had. I began to understand why the Lord is called a rock and a refuge.

Like the Samaritan woman in her moment of beholding, I discovered myself to be held in love by the Lord. That was a threshold moment, and though I still had a long road to travel, I was given the courage to begin taking a few feeble steps forward on my pilgrimage. Jesus' assurance meant that, whether I can perceive it or not, there *is* somewhere to go from here. The pages of my book may be blank, but their blankness is now no longer a symbol of despair's emptiness but of hope. Somehow though nothing changed in my circumstances, everything changed.

Everything changed for the woman at the well, too.

I love the subtle detail of her dropping her old water jar, which represents her old ways of trying to satisfy her thirst on her own. It never did her much good and she won't need it anymore now that she has a well of living water springing up inside of her. That withering way of life is over with. Then, she runs off with a new song of joy pouring from her lips. Those lips had been so parched; every song had dried up. But she goes to the town knocking on doors, singing, "Come meet this man!"

Our Own Worst Enemies

Scripture says "God is love" (1 John 4:8) but the broken heart of humanity flips the phrase, asserting instead that "love is god." There's a world of difference in that subtle reversal. "Love is god" makes our wandering, confused passions the means of navigating a bewildering world. *I am prone to wander, Lord, I feel it!* On the other hand, "God is love" means that love is an actual concrete person with a face; this person, Jesus, is our fixed, steady, unconfused point of reference. When Jesus says "Follow me," it means we're not doomed to be forever trapped in the closed system of our sin. There's a Way out. The woman at the well had followed that subtle reversal of *love-as-god* to its throttling, thirsty end, like we all do. But *the heart is deceitful above all things*.[5] Once her loves had left her at the bottom of a dried-up well, she met the Lord, and found a spring of Living Water, the Fount of Every Blessing.

So why do we cause ourselves so much trouble? Well, I learned how true it is that we tend to be our own worst enemies. The world avoids the face of Jesus because it prefers the darkness, because its deeds are evil.[6] That's how Jesus explained it to Nicodemus, who was drawn to the light of Jesus' face in the dark of night—but not everyone is drawn. Many work to deface or disregard Jesus. Others, like the woman at the well, are afraid to look. Others don't bother to look because they lack the imagination—they can't imagine that God could ever possibly be happy to see them.

We're all longing to have our very existence affirmed in love; our hearts are forever asking questions like "Is it good that I'm here at all? Would anyone miss me if I weren't?" and the corollaries, "Am I only valuable insofar as I prove useful to others? Would anyone want me if I had nothing to offer them?" Those are sad thoughts, and common as clouds. But the good news really is good; the Lord has made the light of his face to shine upon us. And what is a "shining face"? It's a *smiling* face that is bright with gladness, and Jesus is that face; he has come to make clear that our Creator's loving affirmation of humanity at its outset in Eden still stands. Our Father loves dearly those whom he has made, considers the simple fact of their existence a gladdening thing, and longs to rescue them from every species of death that has put asunder what he has always dreamt of seeing joined in Christ.

---

[5] Jer 17:9
[6] John 3:19

The Samaritan woman's story is our story too. She is the whole human race. We've all been hurt by others and done our share of hurting them too, only to return with an empty water jug. But this woman urges us to keep turning our faces towards God, who has made "the light of the knowledge of God's glory"[7] appear in this world in the face of Jesus. It is only in that face, in the fathomless wells of his loving eyes, that our thirst can truly be met. Only the light of his face can shed light on the truth about us: that we are his Beloved.

That all sounds great, doesn't it? But it has not been the easiest story to sit with. I'd have preferred John 9, where the man born blind is told that his suffering isn't his fault. That would've been nice. But in the story I was asked to dwell in, Jesus lovingly, if bluntly, asks the woman at the well to face her own failures. Before she'll be able to see his face clearly, she'll have to face her own sin. She wriggles, changes the subject, plays religious trivial pursuit, and so on. But the cat's out of the bag. When she finally risks turning to face him, it's with the knowledge that Jesus is under no illusions about her. And yet. Yet he looks at her like *that*. He looks at her in the nakedness of her shame over her very real sin, and she can't help but sing for joy. In fact, she writes this little fact into the lyrics of her song, "Come see the man!" What man? The one *"who told me everything I ever did"* (John 4:29).

The big surprise ending of this encounter is not Jesus pretending like she is a virgin bride. Jesus is too realistic for that. The surprise is that in full view of everything she ever did (and everything done to her) he freely gives her a look of such love that she feels like a virgin again. Because she *is*. Jesus' love is in no way blind; his is an all-seeing look. Being seen by him in this way opens her eyes to good possibilities for herself that she had long ceased imagining could ever be. The most beautiful chapters of her story are still to be written. God's dream for her can still come true.

---

[7] 2 Cor 4:6

But getting to that point isn't so easy. The journey of facing the evil in the world, the evil done to us, and the evil that we have done, is necessary if we're to face Jesus as we truly are. Jesus is no trespasser; he will only heal what we allow him to touch. The more truthful we become in facing our sin, grief, and fear, the more of ourselves becomes touchable as we turn to face Jesus, whose face sheds a light that both reveals and heals. A liar can't be touched because what he presents isn't really him. *Until you tell the truth, you can't be touched.* We must be willing to show up to reality. I think this is part of what Jesus is getting at when he tells the Samaritan woman that the Father is not all that interested in whether he's worshipped on this or that mountain. Rather, the Father is seeking people willing to really show up in "spirit and truth." It's almost as if he's saying to her and to us, "I know the real you is in there somewhere hiding behind so many protective layers, but you can come out now. It's safe."

The nitty-gritty details of my own experience aren't really the point here, because this isn't really an album about my marriage or divorce, but rather about what it's like to be a human learning to turn and face Jesus in spite of all the baggage that gets in the way.

This assurance of his love is the only thing that can get us through the process of honesty. By sitting down at the well and striking up a conversation with the deeply broken, he makes clear that he's already made up his mind about us; he was seeking our faces long before we ever sought his. *Belovedness is actually our starting point*; from there we are given the courage to be vulnerable in a process of facing ourselves that would otherwise be too devastating to endure. For those of us who can't tell the difference anymore between who God says we are and the names our Enemy has called us, and those for whom losing what we've become, even if it is miserable, feels like it will kill us, Jesus interrupts to clarify. When making contact with the truth of our own guilt and woundedness feels like giving our pain the final say, Jesus steps into the world to bring a better and more final word, ultimately at the cross.

At the cross, the dying face of Jesus leaves no room for doubt about whether or not we are loved. *I don't owe jack to confusion, now Love has come and made himself so clear.*

A Welling-up of Song

In the end, there's no way around learning to entrust ourselves to Jesus in the very place where it is the last thing we feel able to do. That's painful. Who wants to feel all that pain? I didn't. However, it was in that moment of facing Jesus by the hearth that a new song began to well up within me. It was just the tiniest bit of moisture seeping up through the bare ground, but over the following five years it would slowly gather to a tune enough to carry in a bucket.

St. Augustine says that only the lover sings; only the soul that bravely takes a drink from the Living Water has a chance of discovering a full-throated song that simply must overflow if her joy is to be complete. But here's the kicker: *only the one who dares to look the Lord full-on in the face finds out the shocking good news.* The Samaritan woman leads the way for us. Though it wasn't easy for her either, she risked it, and her life speaks like the old song: "How can I keep from singing?"[8]

Scripture says, "For with you is the fountain of life; in your light we see light" (Ps 36:9). In the light of Jesus' face, she is lit like a candle, and she goes door to door singing, "The Lord *has* made the light of his face to shine upon us. Come and see!" For,

> "Streams of mercy never ceasing
> Call for songs of loudest praise"![9]

Matthew Clark
September 2021

---

[8] Anonymous author, "How Can I Keep from Singing?" Public Domain.
[9] Robert Robinson, "Come Thou Fount of Every Blessing." Public Domain.

1

Looking for You

"We all are born into the world looking for someone looking for us."
Curt Thompson, *The Soul of Shame*

"But the LORD God called to the man, 'Where are you?'"
Gen 3:9

I was probably four years old at the time. I had chased my brother Sam, who is seven years older, and one of his buddies out into the trees behind our house in Ackerman, Mississippi, where, if you walked far enough through the woods, you really did end up at our grandmother's house.

I was a typical tag-along nuisance, and the bigger, faster boys easily left me in the dust. After moping around a while, I started to make my way back towards the house. Then I tripped and fell, knocking or scraping something badly enough to make me cry.

It's funny what you remember. What I remember most strongly was feeling so pitiful and sad about being alone and left out, that I decided in my little boy mind to lie on the ground and cry until someone came to find me. Surely, I thought, I'd be missed and looked for. Someone would come scoop me up. Any minute now.

I lay on the ground at the roots of the trees, and waited. The afternoon drifted into evening as the chirrups and bird-chatter of day gave way to the croaks and creakings of night.

No one came looking.

I gave up eventually, and limped back (very dramatically, I'm sure) to the house, where no one seemed to have noticed I had been gone. Later, I came to relish the fact that our parents didn't hover, and having spent hours upon glorious hours alone in the woods is something I treasure from my childhood. But at that moment, I didn't want to be alone. I wanted to look up and find myself looked for.

This happened long before the legion voice of shame had a chance to take up residence in my life. As Andrew Roycroft's essay makes clear, shame has a way of convincing us that not only is no one missing us, but we were never worth missing in the first place. But those devils are all diabolical liars seeking to put asunder what God always intended to be wedded in perfect, fear-dissolving love.

What if, after believing those diabolical lies until they'd hardened like an asphalt crust over pastureland, a tiny green-leafed question worked its way up through some oily crack in the blackness? What if you found out that something impossibly good was true?

Looking for You

What if you found out someone had been looking,
Looking for you the whole time, the whole time?

Tell me, do you feel forgotten?
Tell me, do you feel like a throw-away
Left last in line and never picked to play?
You're wondering if your prayers have ever made it
Past the ceiling

Seems like I recall a story
Seems like I recall a son who left
Flat turned his back on everyone who cared
He never would have guessed that every day since then
The Lord was searching

I'm telling you there is a friend who
Loves you at your worst
And he is searching everywhere

Child, when your heart gets broken
Child, when your heart gets stolen by
Thieves in the valley, covered up in lies
God is out there digging where the rest gave up
On the treasure

A Stranger on the Road
Andrew Roycroft

Shame never supplied a roadmap, insisting you follow the course they set for you. (Shame is plural because, like Legion, its voices are many.) With terrifying skill, Shame carried you away, along the high-hedged lanes of skewed logic, out onto a footway where thought was no longer needed, only raw feeling, guilt, a hung head, and a heavy heart. Shame shared little about your destination, insisting it was more effective to keep you travelling than talk about arrival or belonging. Shame invited you to rest in roadside lodges where the table was only ever set for one, where the rooms were windowless, with single beds and a trickling excuse for running water. Each day, Shame gave you an early wakeup call, reminding you of why you belong on the road and not at home, instilling in you again the fact that you are broken.

Occasionally Shame would lose their focus and you could snatch a reprieve, branching off the footway and down some back road, where birds dared to sing the day, and where the sunlight offered a brief embrace. You met with others who had found this way. Together you drifted along pine-needled paths, into the hush of heavy canopied woodland, finally finding a clearing where you sat together, just half a dozen, and soaked up your surroundings. At times you talked with one another, but never about your shared master, Shame. You spoke in words with well-rounded edges, careful, politic, never fully opening up your heart or probing the hearts of others. At first you welcomed their offer of sharing in a common cup, but you learned that the coolness of that water in your mouth was bitter to your gut.

Soon you were back on the footway, driven there by sulking Shame, who was affronted at your boldness in seeking fellowship. While the road only carried you in one direction, the lane opposite seemed like a different world. The travellers there were well-dressed, their heads held high, engaging constantly with one another, but never with those on your side of the footway. In the earliest days of your journey, you tried to stop some of these travellers, forlornly hoping that you might be able to switch sides and go with them. Only one ever stopped to give you the time of day, but his demeanour was aloof and condescending. He would tell you nothing of his destination, nor even his name. From then onwards, the mere sight of those other travelers wounded you more and more deeply, and you never crossed to speak with them again.

Once at dinner time in the roadside lodge you were approached by a stranger who hustled a seat alongside your table and asked to enjoy your company. Starved for days of any conversation, you accepted, gratified when your fellow traveller ordered a bottle of the finest wine and much better food than you had eaten so far on your travels. The conversation made your heart leap, touching the nerve of your relationship with Shame, proffering sympathy and commiseration about your bitter journey. At the end of the evening, when your senses were slick with red wine, the stranger invited you to share an en suite room in the upper sections of the lodge, far from the bustle and clamour of the roadside. You hesitated for a moment, but Shame suddenly appeared in the dining room urging you to accept the offer, to allow yourself this luxury. Blushing, you gratefully accepted. But the next morning you were awakened by Shame ceaselessly raining blows on your head. The double bed had been stripped while you slept, and the room furnished with old photos of your past. Your companion left the room, eyes now hard and black, face alive with gleeful reproach on you and on your history.

Years into the monotony of the journey, you became disturbed by the presence of a stranger who seemed to be following you. He would appear in the same village inns you chose, and sit alone nearby, quietly eating his meal and occasionally watching you. There was something in his eyes that made you squirm, but not with concern that you would be harmed again. There was a burning benevolence in his gaze, a fervent emotion that for a moment looked like something stronger than love.

On one such night, someone knocked on the door to your room. Quickly lifting the peephole cover, you saw that it was Shame, come to speak to you. For a moment, you felt both relieved and disappointed that it was not the stranger at your door. Then Shame rushed into the room, throwing all of the bolts on the door in a panic. They bade you sit, and asked in hurried tones, "Have you seen the stranger following you these weeks?"

Heart leaden, you swallowed and responded, voice constricted and hoarse: "Yes . . . yes, I have. Who is he?"

"Never mind his name!" shouted Shame. "All you need to know is that you must never speak with him, and certainly never listen to him. He is a liar who peddles stories about different roads. He's dangerous; he's a predator; he means you great harm."

"He looks kind," you muttered.

Shame moved towards you with fearful speed, taking you by the throat, and spat words into your face that felt like thorns. "You have done enough damage already, don't you think? Listen to these words: NEVER speak with this man. I will kill you very slowly if you do." Then Shame took a seat at the end of the bed, demanding that you lie down, but wakening you every hour to remind you of your past.

With each day's travel, your consciousness of the stranger grew. The more you increased your pace, the more closely he followed behind you, at times within touching distance. With the death that Shame threatened constantly looming in your mind, you would mingle with crowds of travellers, or cross lanes on the footway, but still the stranger was there. At night you began to avoid the popular lodging towns, delving deeper and deeper into the badlands, choosing hostelries where the air stank with transgression and reproach. Here there was only bread and water, eaten furtively at the bar. Other travellers would steal your bread or spit in your water, and the threat of violence hung in the air with stinging force. You were sure that such a place would shake the stranger, but time and again you would see him at the far end of the bar, often handing his rations to other travellers with a look of pity and concern.

One night at a hostel, the rain guttering and pooling through the bottom of the ill-conceived door, the stranger approached and stood right beside you. Your mind lurched and heaved, all emotion and no thought. Unthinkably, he spoke your name. You had not heard it on another's lips for what felt like a lifetime.

"How do you know my name?" you stammered, shocked that he had broken breath with you.

"Our Father gave it to you," he said in a voice both soft and capable of great power.

"Fath—" you choked on the word, and abandoned trying to say it again. "He is a distant memory to me; I cannot think of him."

"But he thinks of you, and he has sent me to look for you, to speak with you, and to bring you home. He loves you, and on the very day you left, he sent me to seek you." The stranger's tone was tender, trembling with emotion.

You sat in silence for a long while, crumbing the hard loaf onto the bar. At last, you responded, "What is your name?"

"Immanuel," he replied, and the word wounded and healed you all at once.

"Oh, please!" you gasped, tears flowing. "Please take me home now! I'll go with you."

"I will take you home," Immanuel offered, "but you must trust me for the journey. It won't be easy, but its outcome is sure. Meet me here in the morning before dawn, and we will set out."

Retiring to your room, which was furnished like a cell, you lay on the hard, flea-infested bed. Your heart was glowing. *Home. Your name.* Those words had not been spoken with tenderness for longer than you could remember. You closed your eyes and began to drift into sleep.

Shame was suddenly at your side, their eyes aflame with malice. Without a word, they pulled you from where you lay. With no sound from their lips they began to beat you, mechanically and efficiently, kicking and punching you with greater force than you thought possible to endure. Finally, as a rooster began to presage the dawn, they stood above you. With stunning calmness, they stamped on your ankle, shattering it with a single blow. "See where you can walk with Immanuel now," they snarled, taking their customary seat at the end of the bed.

Surprised that the promised death was not now yours, you lay face-down and panted into the grimy floor. Pain wracked your entire body. Your ankle pulsed and throbbed, sending shockwaves along the whole limb. You clambered on to your one good leg, feeling every place where Shame had wounded you. Groping in the darkness for the door handle, you limped and lumbered out of that place.

Immanuel was at the bench when you shambled in. Rushing to your side, he propped you up with a strength that belied his slight frame.

"Don't worry," he soothed, speaking your name again. "I have strength enough to get you home. We will not take the footway anymore, but must go by the back roads. The journey will be shorter but much harder than you imagine."

Together you left the hostel, and the dawn seemed endlessly delayed as you hobbled beside Immanuel, leaning heavily on his shoulder. The road was serpentine, populated by miscreants and devil-faced men whose gaze fell on you with a malice and constancy that made dread creep across your chest. Shame seemed to scream at you from each of their faces. The farther you travelled, the more closely the darkness seemed to cling to you. Immanuel's face was set firmly on the road ahead, and your clumsy limp did not seem to perturb or burden him.

After what seemed like days of walking, you arrived at another hostel, a hellish prison of a place with no lights in the windows. Immanuel ushered you inside, helping you into a ragged chair beside a soot-smudged window. From below, in the basement, you could hear howls and shrieks, as though souls were being tormented. Immanuel shuddered, and then spoke, his voice tight and firm. "You must wait here," he said. "Don't leave this room, and do not try to light any candles. I will return soon." Opening a door to the cellar, he disappeared into darkness.

You burst into uncontrollable tears, horror and terror and tiredness rubbing salt into your pain-racked body. Where had he gone? What was he doing? How long would he be? On the sill at the darkened window sat a candle and a box of matches. You longed for some light, but remembering Immanuel's words, you resisted the temptation to use them.

Time passed, and curiosity gave way to the grip of fear. Through the floor beneath you, the howls and crowing from the cellar seemed to intensify. You now felt parched for light, famished for even a faint glimmer. Without further thought, you struck a match and lit the stubby candle. Its light was surprisingly far-reaching, and the room it revealed was diabolical.

The walls were covered with photos from your past, cruelly altered by the unmistakable hand of Shame. The garden where you had once played in the presence of your Father was overgrown with knotweed, its roots fissuring the once-warm brick walls that enclosed it. Family portraits, once redolent with mutual love, had been cunningly altered, your image scratched out of them, and your Father's expression changed to one of rejection and disgust. On and on the pictures stretched, each one engraved with pain, regret and impotent sadness. Your mind reeled and raced, your heart surging, your head spinning. Spreading pain strangled your throat and your voice. Shame was dealing the death they had promised, irretrievably splintering your soul.

You woke with a start, no longer in the hostelry but in your Father's garden. You had been laid down on a bench with a light blanket draped across you. The pains in your joints were gone. Blinking more fully awake, you saw Immanuel at your side. He looked different now, seasoned in some way. His eyes held the same searching, loving fire that you observed on first seeing him. You began to speak, but he raised his finger to his lips in hush. His hand was scarred deeply, but beautifully, his bronzed forehead stippled as though by thorns. "There will be time for talking," he said, "and singing, and laughing, and dancing. First, though, we must dine."

Taking you by the hand, he led you to a large mead hall that adjoined the garden. Countless places had been set at the long tables; Immanuel led you to yours, stopping to pull your seat out for you. "Our Father is here already, and is looking forward to our meal together," he said softly. "Many others will join us."

As Immanuel moved away, your eye fell on your place setting. Embossed on the white card was your name, followed by five words:

LOVED – LOST – SOUGHT – FOUND – HOME.

2

Every Beauty

*"A poem begins with a lump in the throat;
a homesickness or a love sickness."*
Robert Frost

*"When I consider your heavens,
the work of your fingers,
the moon and the stars,
which you have set in place,
what is mankind that you are mindful of them,
human beings that you care for them?"*
Ps 8:3–4

This was a big deal.

I had made up my mind to send flowers to a girl I liked, and the next day at school I'd get to find out what she thought about it. What she thought about *me*, I mean. Would she be shocked because she hadn't even noticed me? If that was the case, she might like the flowers well enough, but leave me to wilt in the corner. But maybe, just maybe, my intuition was on target. *Maybe* I was picking up on the right vibes. *Maybe* she had been silently, ever-so-slyly asking for these flowers. And not just from anybody, but from me.

As a shy fourth grader I already had plenty of capacity for worried romantic imaginings. I knew, even then, that to hold out a bouquet of flowers to a girl is to put your heart on the line, but it was worth the vulnerability. And the aching knot that inevitably forms in the stomach was part of the fun.

Recently, I packed up Vandalf the White (my converted camper-van) and drove to Rocky Springs, Mississippi. Rocky Springs is an abandoned town from the 1800s whose ruins are situated along the old Natchez Trace. A little Methodist congregation still meets once a month in the only building still standing: an ancient red brick church with a graveyard where honey bees buzz from a hidden recess in a cedar.

I'd gone out there to escape the light pollution and catch the Perseid meteor shower. My alarm woke me at 1 a.m., and I stationed myself in the deep night under starlight. I waited and watched. One shooting star became two, three, ten, twenty. By 5 a.m., when I finally turned in for the night, I had seen seventy-seven shooting stars!

Samwise Gamgee found hope in the sight of a single star piercing the sooty cloud rack of Mordor and I'd been given a superabundance. All that beauty felt like a declaration of intent, a kind of lover's proposal, all those stars tingling like bright bells down the ringing halls of time, as if time itself might be an aisle for a bride.

But those halls rang with a strange quietude—as if behind all that beauty was someone with an aching knot in their own stomach, silently awaiting my response. *My* response? Could this whole world—this whole vast cosmos, in fact—be a carefully arranged bouquet held out in vulnerable hope by a Great Lover?

If that was true, then the persistence of the Perseids, alongside every other beauty, was proof that, in spite of all the soot that clouded my heart, God had not withdrawn the proposal. He was still down on one knee, and any one of us at any time could still say "Yes."

Every Beauty

Think of the world the LORD has made
As if it were a lover's bouquet
Held out just to make the heart of God
Plain in every beauty that you see
Every star in the sky
Every kind look in someone's eyes
He is calling out to you
Through the good things he's speaking through

Maybe there's a story that you've heard
That opens up an aching in your heart
Where something like a light behind a door
Has made it through the cracks to where you are?
There's a lump in your throat
And the tears come to your surprise
Like there's someplace that you belong
With someone who loved you all along

Every heart born on earth is so thirsty to be loved
But every heart gets so beat up 'til it's lost out in the hurt
And the heartbeat of our song as we try to get it back
Is same tune that the Lord is singing back to us

Now, there is a highway through this world
That opens like an aisle for a bride
And you can hear the song the groom has made
Threading through the patchwork of our days
There's Table like a ring
And a King down upon one knee
Hear the blood and body speak:
"Make the whole world our wedding feast"

Eggardon Hill
Lanier Ivester

"Here, take my floppy hat," Jenny said, plucking a red straw affair from a peg by the door.

"And for God's sake, don't forget your torch this time," Richard growled. "You don't want us sending out a search party should you decide to drop in at The Three Horseshoes on your way back."

Richard and Jenny were our hosts for the sunlit fortnight my husband, Philip, and I were spending in Dorset, and although our acquaintance had originated with a rental agreement on the little converted cider barn west of their orchard, within moments of our first meeting we had known ourselves to be in the presence of kindreds. Already Richard had invited us up to the farmhouse for gins and tonics ("A couple of long ones for the short walk home," he'd muttered with a little smile, dropping one lonely ice cube into each of our room-temperature drinks), and Jenny and I had connected over gardens and dogs and the novels of Elizabeth Goudge. Matilda, their Fox Red Labrador, was a frequent visitor to our cottage, often darting off again with one of Philip's shoes, or dropping one of Jenny's gardening gloves on the doorstep as a friendship offering.

While Richard possessed a classical Englishman's ardor for his scepter'd isle, Jenny had cultivated a rambler's passion for this particular green and gold corner of it. Philip and I had come to rely heavily upon her recommendations for the best walks and views. And today, her recommendation was emphatically Eggardon Hill. "It's so clear you'll be able to see all the way to Dorchester," she told us. "Or perhaps even the sea. Yes, I think you should go to Eggardon Hill."

"Eggardon Hill" was not a name to inspire awe, or even the most judicious flight of fancy. Nevertheless, we were given to understand that it was something of a local treasure, dominating the chalk uplands east of Bridport like a great, green, sleeping giant. We had skirted it on the A35 before tunneling down into one of the dark, tree-lined lanes with which the countryside is threaded in this part of the world—but a flying glimpse by car is no substitute for the respectful approach à pied. Besides, Philip and I were of the persuasion that the only way to really get to the heart of a place was to walk it, as thoroughly and as merrily as we could.

The wide brim of Jenny's hat drooped at a sultry angle in the late morning warmth, but it was welcome all the same, if entirely incongruous with my jeans and walking shoes. *The very best kind of day*, my heart sang, *and the very best kind of walk!* as we tramped along, water bottles bumping against our knees and a warm wayside lunch tucked into my field bag. Up into the village of Powerstock (with a wave for The Three Horseshoes) and then down again into one of those meandrous lanes, redolent with the hollow-damp aroma of ferns and lush verdure—the very scent of the color green and the essence of England itself. The banks on either hand mounted high as if to close over our heads, and far above, the ivy-clad trees entangled themselves in a fond embrace, affording only the occasional glimpse of a late-summer sky.

On a sunny upland we paused for our lunch—baguettes stuffed with local ham and Dorset Blue Vinney, salt and vinegar crisps, and apples from an obliging orchard—before pressing on, picking up the trail of a dismantled railroad and following the public footpath right through the barnyard of a working dairy farm. The whole day was so lovely, so entirely in keeping with all our ideals of *holiday* that I forgot for the moment that our wanderings had an aim. It wasn't until the Hill came into view, just beyond the final farm gate, that I fully measured the scope of our quest. Imposing, yes, massive and steep, but also something more—something ancient and unassailable and wise.

We stood for a moment in appreciative silence, then hauled ourselves up the winding lane to the foot of the Hill itself, veering off into a thin, but well-trodden track to begin the scarped ascent. Eggardon Hill had been an Iron Age hill fort, and a Bronze Age barrow before that, and as we clawed and scrabbled our way up the grassy slope—all but on our hands and knees at times—I couldn't help but think of Dante and Virgil struggling up the purgatorial mountainside:

> "My son," said he, "drag thyself onward—look! . . ."
> His words were such a goad,
> I strained to follow, and with desperate pressure
> Crawled on—crawled up—and on the terrace stood.[10]

Reaching the summit at last, we threw our breathless selves down on the daisy-sprinkled grass, and for a moment Jenny's red hat flopped down over both my eyes, so that all my senses were trained upon the force of the wind darting over and about our tired bodies. A moment more and it seemed to blow right into me, scattering my weariness like a flurry of dried leaves. I sat up, clamping a hand over the crown of the hat to keep from losing it altogether, then I scrambled to my feet, standing wordless and open-mouthed beside my husband.

---

[10] Dante Alighieri, *The Divine Comedy*, trans. Dorothy Sayers (London: Penguin, 1955), 96.

For miles and miles the countryside opened out below us—hedged fields and steep, grassy slopes, church steeples rising from the quilted folds of far-off hills and thatched cottages embowered in apple trees. An ocean of green fading gently into distant blue hazes, and from away to the south, so mystical and remote it seemed almost the stuff of "fairie lands forlorn," came the bright, pearlescent flash of the sea.

The beauties of Dorset had been summoning tears to my eyes since we first arrived, but this view, this sunlit, windswept moment, summoned something deeper still. It swelled from the marrow of my soul, bursting open the cupboards of my mind, sweeping clear the very corners of my heart. Searing as grief, winged as joy, it brimmed to the surface as an instinctual reply, two whispered words snatched away by the wind yet reverberating silently in the golden air.

Thank You.

There was nothing else to say, nothing to do but to receive such sublimity as the gift I suddenly knew it to be. It reminded me of the time, early in our marriage, when we had gone searching for C.S. Lewis's Golden Valley amid the rolling hills of Herefordshire: I had been sad because the day was gloomy, with sullen mists punctuated by fits of rain, and though the verges of the lane were laced with fool's parsley and "white with May," my heart had sunk a little at every bend. For ten years I'd dreamt of coming upon this place in the sunshine. It had been a symbol of sorts, a deeply personal image of my hopes for a future characterized by goodness and saturated with mercy. I knew God was good, of course—an irrefutable token of that goodness was seated across the car from me. And I knew that weather like this was the very thing that made England such a green and pleasant land in the first place. Nevertheless, longing flailed within, a wild bird beating its wings against the walls of my heart. We might never pass this way again. And it just seemed so unbearable that all my visions might be snuffed out by this soggy reality.

Suddenly, emerging from a stand of sentinel oaks and beeches, the view opened up, and in that same moment the sky opened as well, as if torn asunder by an eager hand. Sunlight rained from ragged bits of blue sky, piercing the landscape with golden shafts, while shadows of the shining clouds pursued one another over the verdant hills and down into the misty hollows. Light fairly rippled over the scene, glorifying everything it touched, and I caught my breath over a sob.

Philip stopped the car and I leapt out, hardly thinking but to inhabit that radiance, to let its benediction fall full upon my tear-stained face and upturned head. Running down the lane a few paces, my tears turned to laughter; the bird had escaped the cage of my heart, but the bird *was* my heart, and both were homing towards the Love beyond all this beauty, the author of this light and the shepherd of these shadows. It was as though the whole vista was spread out as a banquet, inviting us to feast on God's particular goodness and to affirm that his love was indeed loveliest when glimpsed through the veil of our own tears.

I returned to the car with a sober little smile and took my seat at Philip's side.

"I know," I said quietly, "that God loves us very much."

It was not the first time that the love of God had hailed me through the beauty of the natural world. There had been cold, clear starlit nights of my youth when, sitting at my open window I had sensed a brooding tenderness beyond the velvet of a midnight sky. There had been crystalline dawns in which the loveliness of my neighbor's dew-wet garden had enveloped me in an affection I scarcely had a name for. I was an imaginative girl—in today's parlance, "highly sensitive"—so it might seem a matter of course that I'd receive such moments and treasure them long afterward as indicative of a particular, if inarticulable, grace. But, unlike Eggardon Hill and the Golden Valley, they did not come when I was already on the cusp of sublimity, in holiday mode and actively hoping to be "surprised by joy." They stole into the everyday fabric of my suburban life, plucking my sleeve with the beauty right in front of me—the hush and wonder of a rare Southern snowfall; the shrill, exhilarating cries of migrating cranes; the corresponding joys of the first gardenia and the first hint of wood smoke in the air—illuminating the quotidian with the light of the divine.

Of course, I had neither the language nor the experience to identify it as such at the time. But beauty, I intuited, was a conduit of God's love, held out with all the grace of a heavenly courtier. Many of my profoundest experiences of that love, however, were preceded by the overwhelming conviction that I was completely unworthy of it. Like George Herbert's guest, bidden welcome at Love's feast, I often drew back from the gulf of God's grace, "guilty of dust and sin." My youth was marked by innocence and characterized by joy, shot through with moments of such an intense awareness of the presence of God as to hold me rapt and thankful for days. But it was also marked by an inverse sense of shame, so native it never occurred to me to question its presence or validity. A sheltered upbringing made space for ideals to form and imagination to flourish—for which I am eternally thankful. But it also made space for a deep-seated disquiet to spread, a self-condemnation that seemed to be only an echo of God's general disappointment with my unperfected state. If I made myself squirm over my inadequacies, what must God really think of me? And how was I ever to earn his favor?

Such misconceptions of grace took me years to unravel. But beauty was ever the glad witness tugging on the thread of maladaptive belief. One night, late in my teens, I begged my parents to let me stay home from evening service at church. I was tired, I told them, which was true, but not in the way I let them think. My soul was tired, young as it was, weary of inner battles and endless striving. I wanted to pray away all my doubts and dark thoughts, but as soon as the family station wagon eased out of the driveway and lumbered down the street, I sat at the bend of the front walkway instead, elbows on knees, chin in hands, an utter dejection of nineteen-year-old despair. I was too exhausted to pray; too spent from fending off the blows of my harsh inner critic to do more than simply exist amid all the loveliness of that early summer evening.

I should have gone to church with my family. I should have more faith. I should be a better person.

It was June, and the lawn and new leaves were still startling in their first freshness. A brown thrasher launched his vespers anthem from the top of the magnolia tree, and high among the pines the cool breath of evening stirred, fanning off the humidity of the day. I looked up wearily, above our neighbor's low brick house, above the power lines, above the pines, and my breath caught in my throat. There, mounting and pillaring amid a fading sky, the colors of the sunset were staining the clouds with every gradation of coral and salmon and rose, fading into tints of lavender and pale violet. Most striking of all, the setting sun struck their ramparts with gleaming banners, an aureate fortress awash with sudden glory.

It was not only beautiful—*it was saying something.* That airy fortress, I realized, was just like my heart: a fragile, vaporous defense around my guilt and my shame. But God's grace had invaded that shame with overwhelming and unconditional love; I knew in that moment that this was what I was meant to understand, that this was what I had stayed home from church to see and hear in the trustworthy "second book" of God's lovely old world. His love was more real than my perceived unlovableness, his commitment to me more relentless than my worst feelings could ever be. He had stormed the castle of my soul with tenderness and conquered my heart with *his* beauty. That particular sunsct—on an ordinary day, in an ordinary place—washed over my inner life, extinguishing for the moment any idea of earning God's favor. It was impossible—what's more, it was *done*. The whole experience was so extraordinary, I spent the rest of the night trying to write a poem about it, all but exhausting my thesaurus over the attempt to capture that beauty and the gift it had borne.

The fact is, such moments were more than the heights and depths of a sensitive girl. For one thing, I did not find them—they found me, and often at my lowest points. Additionally, they corresponded with something I had already begun to suspect, something I encountered more in the poetry and stories I read than in the sermons I heard at church—namely, that God really does speak to us through the witness of the natural world. "Earth's crammed with heaven," declared Elizabeth Barret Browning; "The world is charged with the glory of God!" proclaimed Gerard Manley Hopkins.

> *The sun, the moon, the stars, the seas, the hills and the plains,—*
> *Are not these, O Soul, the Vision of Him who reigns?*[11]

posed Tennyson, although even our best visions in this life are but "a straight staff bent in a pool," a faulty image of a perfect reality. The whole idea felt a little dangerous at first, almost pantheistic. But the closer I got to it, the more instinctual I found it to be, all but indivisible from my belief in God himself. All of creation was participating in this great interchange of love, and nature was a conductor, allowing that current to flow unimpeded from the unseen world to the seen. Theologians would call it a sacramental ontology—an understanding of reality in which everything matters and everything has a voice. The psalmist insists that the heavens are telling God's story, generally and particularly, that the earth is at once his tender care and his mouthpiece. Peter Kreeft once said that if we could really understand what the sea was saying as its waves curled and thundered onto the shore, over and over again, it would be simply this: *I love you, I love you, I love you* . . . Endlessly, ardently, unconditionally.

---

[11] Alfred, Lord Tennyson, "The Higher Pantheism."

Beauty is the soul's native tongue, and the experience of it one of the ways humans can know they are beloved of God. One April evening, long before Eggardon Hill but well after the Golden Valley, Philip and I were walking across our backyard towards the barn. It was just at that gilded moment when the sun, flinging out its final banners above the horizon touched the treetops with a coronet of gold, and as we stopped to admire it, Philip told me how boys used to train their arrows into that light, longing to see their shaft illuminated with a glory beyond its own grace before it fell to earth once more. "There was probably some prize for it," he said, "but I think the achievement was prize enough in itself." It was just the way of beauty, I thought—of art or of nature, majestic or humble—it lifted the heart along its numinous course, just glancing the realm of the sublime before turning back towards our world. Beauty was not the sublimity—it was an arrow, the servant of something greater, and for now, the arrows were all we could bear. But the memory of that realm remained, and the things the arrows pointed to were true.

We lingered for hours on Eggardon Hill, watching the martins wheel and dart on the billows of air, inspecting the earthworks, wandering over the massive tumuli. Then we walked home a different way, along the old Roman road, which travels a ridge towering high above one of those steep Dorset valleys. There were fresh beauties on every hand: green hills tumbling into dark, wooded combes, the last light of day gilding everything it touched, and a clear, pale sky springing overhead.

I love you, too, Lord, I silently replied as we tramped down into the gathering dusk, companioned, as always, by unwavering goodness and unmerited mercy.

(We did drop in at The Three Horseshoes, by the way. And we did forget our torch.)

3
The Well

"[In the Bible] the betrothal type-scene, then, must take place with the future bridegroom, or his surrogate, having journeyed to a foreign land. There he encounters a girl—the term 'na'arah' invariably occurs unless the maiden is identified as so-and-so's daughter—or girls at a well. Someone, either the man or the girl, then draws water from the well; afterward, the girl or girls rush to bring home the news of the stranger's arrival (the verbs "hurry" and "run" are given recurrent emphasis at this junction of the type-scene); finally, a betrothal is concluded between the stranger and the girl, and in the majority of instances, only after he has been invited to a meal."
Robert Alter, *The Art of Biblical Narrative*

"'For this reason a man will leave his father and mother and be united to his wife, and the two will become one flesh.' This is a profound mystery—but I am talking about Christ and the church."
Eph 6:31–32

If you've ever been to the South Dakota Badlands, you can picture the starkness of that landscape. I don't know what the Judean Desert is like from personal experience, but I imagine it to be as fitting a place for a brokenhearted soul to withdraw as the Badlands were for me. Sometimes you go find a place that looks on the outside like what you feel on the inside.

I drove that nearly 1,200 miles non-stop one night after a hoped-for love fell through. Then I curled up in the fetal position in the trunk of my old Nissan Maxima and slept. I wandered around alone for many days in that cold, bleak, grey-hilled country, having told no one where I was going. I felt so lost, I didn't even want to be found anymore.

One of those mornings, I cried against a retaining wall on a hillside for a while (I know, dramatic), then walked over to the little park café and ordered pancakes and coffee (I've rarely been so dramatically sad as to eschew good food).

Someone once asked me over a late night breakfast at a Waffle House, "Do you know why these folks work here?"

"No," I'd said.

"Because they have to," my friend said.

My park café waitress that morning must've had enough lamentable experience of her own to intuit my sadness, for as I still recall, she was particularly kind to me. Her gentle face and simple friendliness invited me to cross over an invisible threshold. I had gone a long way from home, carried by grief and despair, but there in the midst of that desert country, a kindred heart brought me good things to eat and drink.

I hadn't seen it coming. I hadn't seen anything good coming. I'd stopped looking. And I was in danger of getting used to it: of falling in love with a depression that seemed more substantial than goodness, more real than hope. Until the kind face and presence of a stranger broke that spell with a better spell, a good-spell, a gospel.

The Well: John 4

Jesus, tired as he was, went and sat by Jacob's well
There was no else around, until a woman came from town
She wound her way to him with an empty water jar
She was worn and withered thin, with only thirst to fill her heart

And Jesus asked her for a drink; now, she was used to forward men
So she smiled and played the game, 'cause isn't every man the same?
When he tried to catch her eye, she would not cast a glance
Into the mirror of those depths, where the Living Waters danced

Then he touched a nerve so deep; he said the worst thing he could say
When he laid her sin out plain in the open light of day
But he would not give up yet 'til she could hear him say her name
But she pivoted so quick, just trying to outrun all her shame

With a wave she flung off hope; she dismissed it like a joke
Said, "It'll all work out someday, if Messiah ever shows"
But as she took her jar to go, she turned just quick enough to see
A word well up in Jesus' face, enough to rinse a harlot clean

And I, I want to see it
I want to look him in the eye, I want to look him in the eye
I, I want to see it
See what made that woman sing, see what made that woman sing

Because she dropped her old clay jar, and ran to tell the rest
Of the man who lifted every burden weighing on her chest,
And she sang out clear and clean, like a virgin for her groom,
"Let the whole world come and drink
From the Well who makes what's sad untrue"

Below the Tideline
Théa Rosenburg

"Come, all you who are thirsty, come to the waters."
Isaiah 55:1

I spent this morning at a city park with my youngest daughter, who is five and intoxicated with all the new things she can do. Every few minutes she called, "Mom, look! My feet can reach!" or "Mom, I'm tall enough now!"—as she scaled a rock right at the water's edge, one inaccessible to her a few months ago.

For as long as I've had daughters, I've brought them to this park: a strip of grass along Bellingham Bay with a boardwalk curving out over the water, a quarter-mile long. This morning the tide was out, exposing crescent moons of beach beneath the boardwalk. Blue-black mussels gathered in the folds of the pilings; barnacles starred rocks and driftwood alike.

On one of the beaches, a boy waded into the shallows with a heap of violet sea stars in his arms, which he flung, star by star, back into the water. "Sweetie, don't throw them," his mom said. "Set them down gently."

"I'm rescuing them!" he protested, but he tossed them softly after that. In between the conversation of passing joggers and the burst of a ferry's horn and my daughter skipping along the boardwalk, I could hear the sea stars break the water's surface with a delicate *plip*. I lost sight of them as they slid into the sea.

I have lived most of my life next to Bellingham Bay—not close enough to see the water, but close enough that when the wind skims across the bay, bounds up over the bluff, and tumbles through our yard on its way elsewhere, it saturates the air around our house with a sharp, briny sea-smell. My parents joke that they moved our family here from the Midwest because they wanted to raise us kids in a place we'd never want to leave. I only heard them make that joke when I was in my thirties and raising my own family—by then it was clear that they'd succeeded. But even as a child I knew that I'd never feel fully at home in any place where I could not hear the gulls cry and wheel above our house, or where I did not wake at night to a train whistle, its warning amplified by the still, dark sea.

The ocean is an unknowable presence always on the edge of my awareness: I somehow belong to it but know that it will never belong to me.

On the boardwalk, my daughter made a game of looking over the railing, first off one side of the boardwalk and then the other. For a while we leaned against the railing closest to the beach and watched the boy gather a second armload of sea stars. With the tide out, the bay revealed a few secrets: we could see through the water to the coarse sand below, where oysters clung to the rocks in luminous, ruffled patches. A crab's discarded shell, bright as a marigold, revolved eerily in the slow waves at the water's edge. This morning, the sea seemed open to us—we'd been invited into something hidden at high tide.

But over the railing farthest from the beach, the water was deep, moss green and opaque. Grebes floated on the water, their slender necks like masts and wings tucked tight against their bodies. When one dove down, it disappeared, and we made a game of guessing where the bird would come back up and whether it would have a fish in its beak when it surfaced. It did: the fish's scales flickered blue under the clearing sky before the bird gulped it down.

And then—oh! I gasped aloud and grabbed my daughter's hand. A silhouette broke the surface, just eyes, nose, and whiskers. The seal turned its snout toward us, then toward the family farther down the boardwalk. They gestured and grinned, leaning over the railing—the sea came to us today and we all felt lucky. "Look," I whispered to my daughter, pointing. I tried to turn her so she was facing the seal, but before she could pick out its slim shape in the sea, the seal dove. I caught a last glimpse of its back as it arched up—white and silver, speckled—and then rolled into the green water. I wanted my daughter to have seen it; I felt grateful to have seen it at all. I wanted to know where the seal had gone.

Beyond the boardwalk, there is a boulder I love—a huge, sloping sandstone that at low tide reveals little pockets and caves, benches and tidepools. When I was in college, I would sit there and sketch the islands that ring the bay and the white-crested mountains that ring the islands. This morning we made our way to the rock slowly. For a while my daughter skipped, then she stopped; she was tired and wanted to know when we'd be there. "Almost," I said. "We're close." She lost interest in the water and wearily watched the gravel scrolling beneath her feet.

When we reached the boulder, she lit up: this was worth the walk. We climbed down from the path onto the boulder, and she clambered all over it—up onto this bench, down to that tidepool. She explored the rock thoroughly before settling onto an arm of it near me to count the minute black snails that—we admitted grimly—crunched beneath us every time we moved.

Sitting on this boulder, it felt familiar: I knew its hollows and smooth planes and the grit it left on my hands. But I only knew the part of it that rose above the water—what extended below the tideline remained hidden from me. The barnacles glowed dim and dimmer where the sandstone sloped into the sea.

At the water's edge I am acutely aware that the bay, with its depth and detachment, is indifferent to us. A slippery stone too close to the edge, a sudden wave: the waters the seal finds hospitable would not be so kind to us. While my daughter watched crabs the size and color of olives scuttle from one rock's underbelly to the next, I kept her hand in mine. We were the guests there, and we would be the ones to leave when the tide came in.

And that is the paradox of the sea: we can float upon it or admire what it leaves behind at low tide, but we cannot survive in it. Even with specialized equipment and training, much of the ocean's depths remain inaccessible to us: "No one can now say," Rachel Carson wrote, "that we shall ever resolve the last, the ultimate mysteries of the sea."

The more time we spend here, the more I wonder at this. When we crossed the boardwalk, what swam beneath us? Was the seal alone, or did a bashful companion conceal himself below the water's surface? I am loosely familiar with the green water at the edges of the bay, but what of the bay's center, where the water is deep and implacably blue? If the heavens declare the glory of God,[12] then perhaps the waters declare his incomprehensibility, that knowledge that there will always be more to God than we can see or understand.

The sense that God continues on beyond what we can see— that he is full of surprises—is echoed in the movement within the waters: in the tidepool, a barnacle flicks out a feathered tongue, but we notice only that the barnacle snaps shut again. Out in the bay, something leaps and hits the water with a splash; we look up quickly but see only ripples, expanding over the surface of the water.

---

[12] Ps 19:1

My older daughters have wrestled with this idea lately: Why can't we see God? If he's supposed to be our Father, our friend—why can't we see him? And I am not sure that my answer always satisfies my older children, who like to hear and touch and see the world around them. (My youngest daughter has no such struggle. In a world where there are Dungeness crabs, why shouldn't we have an invisible Father?) But each time my older girls wonder aloud how they're supposed to know a God they cannot see, I point them back to Jesus: he is "the radiance of God's glory and the exact expression of his nature" (Heb 1:3 CSB). Dane Ortlund writes,

> Jesus is the embodiment of who God is. He is the tangible epitomization of God. Jesus is the visible manifestation of the invisible God (2 Cor. 4:4, 6). In him we see heaven's eternal heart walking around on two legs in time and space. When we see the heart of Christ . . . we are seeing the very compassion and tenderness of who God himself most deeply is.[13]

Through the Incarnation, Jesus articulated the incomprehensible nature of God into a visible body. He took on hands—specific hands, with scars and calluses—and used them to build and bless, to comfort and heal. Jesus—the God who spoke to Moses in thunder[14]—took on a particular voice with a particular timbre. With it, he reasoned and rebuked; he prayed and consoled. He summoned those he loved, and they followed.

Jesus arrived not as an unknowable sea but as a well: a body of water limited and directed to one place, for one purpose—to invite us to know his Father. When he became a man with arteries and affections, Jesus translated God's nature into a form we could, in our limited way, understand. "Anyone who has seen me has seen

---

[13] Dane C. Ortlund, *Gentle and Lowly: The Heart of Christ for Sinners and Sufferers* (Wheaton, IL: Crossway, 2020), 133.
[14] Ex 19:19 ESV
[15] John 14:9

the Father,"[15] he said, and it was as though he'd waded into the water and turned it transparent, so that even though we couldn't yet live within it, we could see into it—not into a meticulously staged aquarium, but into a wilderness, a living sea.

But even as Jesus took on the limitations of flesh, he lost none of that bottomless wealth, none of that mystery and abundance he'd had before the Incarnation: he could ask an outcast woman for a drink of water to quench a genuine, physical thirst; he could also offer himself to her by saying, "Whoever drinks of the water that I will give him will never be thirsty again" (John 4:14). Where God's holiness was once no more habitable to us than the open sea, Jesus invites us into it. In him we can know and be known by our perfectly holy, incomprehensible God.

4

Everything but You

"The philosophy of tough love is based on the conviction that no effective recovery can be initiated until a man admits that he is powerless over alcohol and that his life has become unmanageable. The alternative to confronting the truth is always some form of self-destruction. For Max there were three options: eventual insanity, premature death, or sobriety. In order to free the captive, one must name the captivity.
Max's denial had to be identified through merciless interaction with his peers.
His self-deception had to be unmasked in its absurdity."
Brennan Manning, *The Ragamuffin Gospel*

"Where can I go from your Spirit?
Where can I flee from your presence [face]?"
Ps 139:7

"**D**id you eat the cookies?"

"No."

"No?"

"No, I didn't eat the cookies."

In your mind's eye you can already see the little crumb and chocolate-covered face, can't you? I remember lying to my parents as a child, and I remember the burden of it. The dangerous burning of the chest, the vacuous drop of the stomach.

I've been an uncle for a long time, as well, and I know that just as no one needs to teach little children to dance, giggle, or draw, there are darker capacities like lying and manipulation that come innately. And I've been an adult long enough to be forced to admit that those darker capacities have not, as I would like to believe, been outgrown. Instead, they've only grown more subtle and stubborn with time.

And the thing they grow into is hard to look at because of the powerlessness we feel. I knew better than to eat those cookies. I swore I wouldn't. How did I wind up here again for the thousandth time? Good intentions aren't enough to rinse away the crumbs and chocolate, those incessant, obvious clues of our failure. The burden of it is too much.

Lying to other people works—until it doesn't. The most stubborn lie is typically the one we tell ourselves; it often persists long after the truth is obvious to everyone around us. *He's his own worst enemy* is the cliché, until every brush with reality, every proximal approach of truth feels like it'll be the end of us. We scrape, scratch, and bare our teeth like a threatened animal.

There would be no way to tell the story of the Samaritan woman—to tell the human story—without looking honestly at self-deception. The appeal of deception is understandable in a world so heartbreakingly dangerous as ours, because by nature truthfulness requires us to be vulnerable. We need each other, but trust is based on the experience of someone else's truthfulness over time. Initially, lying may seem to preserve safety, but in the long run it dissolves trust, and makes the connection we most long for impossible to maintain.

When trust finally breaks down, who will stay?

When the appetites that I pedestalled as deities have led me to dead-ends, when my lies have left me lonely, who has the will to look on me in the shame of my nakedness and stay? Someone who was never fooled in the first place. Someone who, when they promised to love me, actually knew what they were committing to. No fair-weather friend could handle the disappointment, the betrayal. Then who?

Someone who could *tell you everything you've ever done* and still stay waiting for you by the well in the heat of the day, after everyone else has gone.

Everything but You

When desire itself is soured wine
You will drown in your own wishing well
'Cause when love is god your bleary eyes
Will be the wandering stars you'll travel by

And I was sure that love was leading me
And that God himself had paved the way
But above all else the human heart is deceitful

When I got to the end of the heart that all my loves had emptied
I lost everything, everything, but You

I tore a page out of the holy book
And I tailored words to suit my ears
But I'd spun those clothes like spiderwebs
'Til I was cold and caught in my own fears

'Cause that sugar coat can't cover grief
I learned light does not need dark to see.
Oh, my bones were sown in Eden's soil, don't it make you tired?

Past the gates of hell where I made my bed
I woke up from my dreams to face the truth
That the truth has a Face

When I got to the end of the heart that all my loves had emptied
I lost everything, everything, but You

In the Darkness of Noontide
Adam Whipple

The day is baking. Above the kilned air a blue-bronze sky domes to catch the glare of day-shine spiking off the sun-bleached dust of the road. A dark-skinned man ambles north with a handful of companions into the cross-section of valleys the locals call *Mabartha*, the passage. There is a hole in the noon-lit ground, a well. The man finds a tree to sit under, and hopeful for some refreshment, he sends his friends into the little town to buy bread. There is a glint in his eye; he knows they will be stared at, seen as snobby outlanders, but it's a powerful thing, a disarming thing, to ask another for food.

This is the picture of Jesus traveling through Samaritan country. Even at this point, it raises questions about the extent of his connection to omniscience, to the all-knowing nature of God, Three-in-One. Certainly Jesus valued moments of solitude with the Father. Perhaps this was one of those times. He would have walked much of the morning with his disciples. He might have sent them away for an honest respite, a moment of peace amid many ongoing conversations the men had strung along the road.

Or, did he have a sense of needing to be alone in preparation for what was about to happen? Did he feel and trust the gentle nudge of the Holy Ghost maintaining omnipresent sovereignty while the Son of God was become Son of Man—the Holy Ghost who knew that a lone, thirsty Samaritan woman would not likely approach a well surrounded by over a dozen sweaty men? It seems more than coincidence that Jesus was suddenly by himself.

Seeming every bit the consummate untouchable, the woman arrived at midday, in the heat, after the crowds had removed indoors. She hadn't been expecting anyone else, but there sat this one man. She decided to chance the interaction. Something in his posture, maybe, said he did not intend to be a threat. She carried a small vessel, with a rope attached to it. Setting her chin at the appropriate angle, an angle telling of nonchalance and civility, she stepped towards the well and began to lower the container down. He eyed her work.

"Will you give me a drink?" he said.[16]

There was a particular turn of vowels in his voice, a localized cadence. He was Galilean, and Jewish. Every fiber of her being knew by rote that she was, or should have been, anathema to him. She suddenly felt embarrassed, and not a little vulnerable. Why would such a man even speak to her?

As the story unfolds, John the Apostle reveals more and more of the Samaritan woman's ordeal. Jesus waxes eloquent, and rather bafflingly, about living water, some substance which would keep thirst at bay forever. Sensing an opportunity—though speaking a little wryly perhaps—the woman tells Jesus to give her this water. He responds by telling her to fetch her husband.

"I have no husband," she admits.

Finding her at least truthful about her marital station, Jesus probes further, like a surgeon into a wound.

---

[16] This conversation is from John 4:7, 17-18.

"You have had five husbands," he says to her, "and the man you now have is not your husband. What you have just said is quite true."

Much has been made in sermons of her situation, but in the contemporary parlance of counseling and psychology, the Samaritan woman seems to fit somewhere on the spectrum of codependency, of addiction. We're familiar with this territory. Counselors and therapists have outlined various waystations along paths of grief and addiction. Have we not all dealt with such things in some way? We can easily see that woe and false dependence are intertwined. It's the reason stress-eating becomes a problem. In addition, there comes a point, in journeys both unlooked-for and ill-chosen, where we resign ourselves to our fate. Everything about the woman at the well screams of fatalistic acceptance, of a dwindled will that barely carries on.

Having experienced the hope-shattering of five different failed marriages, it's no stretch to imagine that she had given up, that she despaired of finding someone with whom to share matrimony. While Samaritan culture of that day was markedly different from ours, the rising stars of romantic hope and marital possibility are universal human conditions. Who knows what breathless myths of nuptial bliss were repeated to her prior to her first betrothal? We can assume, at least, that she had some expectation of goodness along the way, but her dreams got destroyed, again and again.

It may seem unfair to call her an addict. What on earth could she be addicted to, after all? She doesn't wear the obvious marks of drunkenness, a common sin of both the past and present. Is she an ensnared postulant at the false altar of sexual sin? Of codependence? The problem here is that sins and legitimate behaviors occupy the same ground. Contrary to the insinuations of the purity culture with which many of us grew up in the American church, sexuality within marriage is invariably imperfect, a country of grace and giving, marred and twisted by human sin. Our blessed interdependence, the way in which the Lord has made us all for each other, also contains the cracks of our own evil. Community becomes codependence; blessing becomes fear; the holiness of giving within God's story-arc of sexuality becomes the faceless taking of an ever-dwindling pleasure. These areas of life are also subject to the claws of addiction, though it's often harder to see. In moments of fear, boredom, loneliness, anger, or fatigue, we run quickly to these good things in place of Christ, falling easy prey to our demons.

So does the woman at the well show some kind of addictive behavior, or is it just her station in life, the way the chips have fallen to someone of her rock-bottom echelon? She had resigned herself to a mere man, after all, not even bothering with marriage this time, keeping as near as her heart could take to someone who could offer the thinnest protection to a person with no legal status. So which is it? Perhaps it's both. Her plight is obvious, but her excited evangelism in town is certainly revealing: "Come see a man who told me everything I ever did," she says of Jesus.

No, he didn't do that. Whether Jesus told her more than was recorded or not, he certainly didn't tell her *everything she ever did*. Her own sense of conscience and complicity in her situation, however, was such that she could not see herself beyond her own sin. To her, she had become nothing more than a walking collection of the wrongs she had done. All that's left to a body at that point is the basest handful of existential principles. We eat, we sleep, we preserve the last astringent mote of humanity out of fear of God or a nearly unbreakable understanding that to kill, even oneself, is wrong. As suicide rates attest, that feeling doesn't necessarily last long.

In such darkness, we want for an out-shaking, a personal explosion that will fling wide the hatches of our own souls to let in the light. Of course it comes when all is lost. In God's character as the Wandering Bard of all creation, He does seem to love telling his own story with an eleventh-hour reprieve. I've lost count of the times when my own prayers were answered just after I had given up praying them for laziness or sheer doubt.

This reprieve looks different for different people. God came to Job in a hurricane of theophany.[17] He did the same for Elijah, but only after He sent delivery from the bakery.[18] Into the Samaritan woman's half-life of despair walked the Light of Life, Jesus himself, in his carpenter-quiet way, so painfully normal that she suspected nothing.

These moments of unexpected balm remind me of Christmas.

Whatever people may say about the Catholic church and its calendars, as someone in the northern hemisphere, I love celebrating the coming of Christ near the winter solstice, what Robert Frost calls "the darkest evening of the year." There, when the sun is farthest away, we ring the bells of the Savior's coming and light candles in the darkness, passing fire from hand to hand in church sanctuaries. The pattern comes again in Jesus' resurrection, the hills and meadows thick with new-springing life.

The Lord, it can't be denied, seems to love a good story in this way.

I suspect it's not just a bardic penchant on his part, but his nature as a shepherd or parent. He has made us as creatures who learn best by experience. For better or worse, the pedagogy of plain speech changes our character much more slowly than the school of hard knocks. I don't want to have to arrive at the abyss to see Jesus. I want Eden, the garden of delights, the halcyon corners flecked with light where the presence of the Lord is constantly obvious and never terrifying. This is the world, though, and the world is infested by my sin. I learn better when the story of Jesus' offered redemption, of my acceptance of his grace, contains the rising ac-

---

[17] Job 38:1
[18] 1 Kings 19:3-9

tion of my most horrid thoughts, words, and deeds. To skimp on such a telling is to belittle God's mercy.

The idol of searching for oneself through romantic love is as ancient as it is false. We cannot be saved from our sins and sinfulness in this way. Making a romantic interest into a demigod, furthermore, is a burden no one ought to put on a spouse. What beloved can bear what C. S. Lewis called "the weight of glory"? And it's only more of the same old nonsense. It's Cain thinking his best option is murder, or Israel smelting a golden calf.[19] The modern gospel of self-improvement, self-acceptance, and self-worth—even through the proxy of a romantic partner—is the same kind of pride.

Jesus did not see the woman's intrinsic worth as something she herself could perceive and grasp. He saw her as only he could see her, and as she needed to glimpse herself: through the lens of him, the Lord of All Creation. What she needed was not self esteem, but what John the Baptist said: "He must become more; I must become less" (John 3:30, paraphrased).

The false gospel of self-acceptance says, "I have intrinsic worth as me, as my true self." The gospel says, "My identity is hid in Christ, hid even from myself; I learn who I am by the path of following, of discipleship." The false gospel of self-acceptance may need Jesus once, for purposes of personal revelation. The gospel adherent needs Jesus constantly and evermore. Like a moon, the heart holds no light of its own, but can only reflect a star. Moons go wandering at their peril. Yet there, even wandering as far as we might from the light of truth, even in the resignation of noonday heat and loneliness, the Light of Truth himself comes looking for us.

---

[19] Gen 4:1-15; Ex 32

5

Trying to Get My Heart Back

"Trauma has shut down their inner compass and robbed them of the imagination they need to create something better."
Bessel Van Der Kolk, M. D., *The Body Keeps the Score*

*"You, Lord, hear the desire of the afflicted;
you encourage them, and you listen to their cry,
defending the fatherless and the oppressed,
so that mere earthly mortals
will never again strike terror."*
Ps 10:17–18

I was alone and the house was utterly silent, while my mind was all the raucous, grinding noise of a rock tumbler. *Click* went the doorknob of the front door, just a room away. Once in high school, in an attempt to sing, I touched my lips to a microphone powered by an ungrounded extension cord. A surge of electricity entered my body, shoved me to the ground, and knocked all the breath out of my lungs. Hearing the *click* of that doorknob sent an instantaneous shock of adrenaline from my head to my toes. Had I not been sitting already, I might have crumpled to the floor. As it was, I froze. All these years later, just typing this out right now puts my nerves on edge, makes it hard to breathe, and my fingers shake.

I knew what the doorknob meant. I knew who was about to be in the house with me.

I wish to God that it were safe to assume you have no idea what I'm talking about, but I know better. You've felt the approach of the trespasser. Who doesn't recognize the footsteps of the invader? It's true that we can be our own worst enemies, but it's also true that we have enemies. Real ones. Some supernatural, and plenty of them flesh and blood.

Old Testament scholar Dr. Sandra Richter was the first person I ever heard explain that one meaning of the term *redemption* in Scripture is rescue from an enemy too strong for us. And I've always loved Jesus' explanation when, after casting out demons, he's accused of doing so by way of demonic power. He says that if the intruder is strong, it'll take an even stronger man to tie him up. The Strongest Man is on the side of those in the grip of the enemy. And like Narnia's Aslan, Jesus is the perfect union of power and goodness. His might to save makes him unsafe to the wicked, while his righteous love means he will never abuse those who cry out to him for redemption.

But trauma has a disheartening effect. We lose heart. It breaks our hearts. We literally lose them, because trauma takes possession of them. The result is that it becomes hard to give ourselves wholeheartedly to much of anything or anyone. Even when we do make contact with someone who has proven trustworthy, the heart we'd like to offer them seems oddly absent. Trauma has absconded with it, and we're left with the question of how to give something away that we no longer possess.

Still, we get little scraps here and there of an old song on the wind that warms our blood. Silver moonlight on the wall surprises us with unexpected beauty in the blackness. Friends make us laugh. Food tastes good. Of course, the trauma is never eradicated from our experience. But now other things happen too—good things—and they begin to accumulate almost imperceptibly like snow to soften and cover the raw red soil.

Perhaps we even come across stories of people like us? They tell hard-to-believe tales of lost treasures in forgotten fields, dug up and given glad gleam again by the sunlight.

Trying to Get My Heart Back

I went down into the cedar brake
Down to where the earthquake
Shook up all the old ways
I used to use to navigate

I went looking for a sign of life
Somewhere past the edge of night
Digging through the trash cans
Trying to find a long-lost friend

Trying to get my heart back
'Cause you can't give away
Something you do not have
Trying to get my heart back

Now I woke up to the silver moon:
Thin enough to squeeze through,
Sneak in past the black dogs,
Climb into my bedroom,

Write upon the dark walls
Something like a love song
It is beating on my windows
So I'm thinking I should hold on

Embracing a New Name: St. Photini
Heidi White

Christians often wonder what happened to the men and women in Scripture whose lives were transformed by Jesus. The Bible offers tantalizing glimpses into moments of divine intervention in the lives of the blind, crippled, wounded, and spiritually oppressed, but we wonder—what happened next? What transpires when somebody "gets their heart back"? And what does that mean for us?

After the ascension of our Lord, the church began the arduous work of transforming itself from a scattered collection of believers into a rooted community of saints. Countless people contributed to the formation of the early church, including theologians, martyrs, missionaries, clergy, and scribes. As the church solidified, it preserved the stories of these early influencers in written and oral tradition. Some of these accounts became integrated into Holy Scripture, but many more can be found in the rich and varied archives of church tradition. Among them is the tale of the Samaritan woman at the well, whose impact extended far beyond the afternoon encounter with Jesus recorded in the gospel narratives and continues today.

Church tradition tells us that the name of the Samaritan woman at the well was Photini. But that was not always her name. Upon rising from the symbolic waters of death, the newly baptized Samaritan woman renounced her former identity and received a new name to correspond with her new identity in Christ. This was not an isolated incident. In fact, nearly all of the convert-saints of the early church are known to us by their baptismal names rather than their given names. This renaming is far more than an empty custom; it reflects the transformative nature of conversion. Once Photini met Jesus, all things—including her very identity—changed. Like all Christians, she was once dead, but is now alive; once lost, now found; once old, now new.

Like the woman at the well, we receive new identities upon entering the communion of the saints. But how does this manifest in our lives? Is our new identity as "Christian" merely an abstract signifier or is there something more practical involved? How do our spiritual identities correspond to our earthly lives? This is a particularly apt question for those of us who, like Photini, bring wounds from the past into our Christian lives. This is also the mystery that haunts Matthew Clark's song, "Trying to Get My Heart Back." Like Photini, the narrator must reckon with the intersection of past misery and an immense present and future grace.

The narrator of the song is at once a specific man and an everyman. His story is a vessel that we can fill with our own stories. Like all lyrical songs, this one is a poem set to music, and like all (good) poems, it contemplates universal mysteries through particular experiences. In this case, the song describes something we recognize: pain, even trauma, from the past. He is "looking for a sign of life somewhere past the edge of night," a respite from "the earthquake" that disrupts the "old ways." But such a disturbance, however redemptive, is excruciating; it feels like "digging through the trash cans." The narrator's search for meaning and hope in the midst of suffering is specific to him, but it also transcends him. We perceive ourselves and the whole world in the haunting crucible of the song.

Like the narrator—and like you and me—the woman at the well was no stranger to sin and suffering. Her life was riddled with pain and grief. Jesus told her, "The fact is, you have had five husbands, and the man you now have is not your husband. What you have just said is quite true" (John 4:18). This is a hard story. We know nothing about the circumstances that brought this terrible brokenness to pass: Was Photini promiscuous in her former life? Deceived? Abandoned? Widowed? Whatever the specifics, she endured profound suffering. And yet she was restored through her encounter with Jesus.

Photini means "enlightened one," which reminds us that past darkness is no hindrance to holiness; rather, it is a backdrop from which the incandescent grace of God shines. We see this reflected in the lyrics of the song, which takes place at night. The words "dark," "black," and "down" describe the narrator's journey, and the darkness is not imagined; the darkness is real. This resonates with all of us because in spite of our feeble efforts to resist, we too cannot escape the crushing weight of grief and trauma. Jesus, "man of sorrows and acquainted with grief,"[20] knew this. Perhaps this is why he reminded this woman of the tragedies of her life, and in the same moment illuminated her with transforming grace. By naming the darkness of her story, Jesus freed her from it, inviting her to renounce the old darkness and embrace a new name: Photini, "enlightened one." Once a child of darkness, she became a child of light.

The song describes an embodied transition from darkness to light. The narrator is alone in his room in the dark. But out of the night, a sliver of light presents itself, "thin enough to squeeze through." Sometimes we need this—a light that does not dazzle or overwhelm, but slips in unobtrusively through the cracks; a Savior

---
[20] Is 53:3 ESV

who does not swoop in triumphantly with a conquering army, but converses kindly over a cool drink of water on a hot afternoon. The infinite God is infinitely small as well as infinitely great. When necessary, he concentrates his power and mercy into the hidden slivers and cracks of our broken hearts. Jesus does not overpower our souls; he heals them. And to our narrator, this precision of gentleness feels "something like a love song."

So it is that we arrive at the crux of the matter, which is love. If the question is "What do we do about our broken hearts?" the answer is always and only to open our hearts to love. Love bears all things, believes all things, hopes all things, endures all things.[21] Such words are worth repeating. Love bears, believes, hopes, and endures all, all, all things, even the rage, remorse, and resistance of the deepest griefs and traumas. Love never fails.[22] After all has been shaken, love alone remains.

But love will not invade; it must be invited. Photini's story teaches us that the greatest tragedy is not to have had five husbands and a lover—such brokenness is frankly par for the course in the unfolding drama of human existence—but to resist love. Better to dig through the trash cans than to ignore the advancing light as it writes a love song on the walls of our hearts. Divine love is gentle but also enduring. It will not encroach, but it will persist. "Here I am! I stand at the door and knock," offers Jesus, and "If anyone hears my voice and opens the door, I will come in" (Rev 3:20). As our narrator discovers, healing love is always "beating on the windows" as the light makes its way towards us, but we too play a part: as the song tells us, we must hold on. And sometimes that is the hardest work of all.

Our sad stories often obscure us from knowing our own hearts. Indeed, the wounds of our lives can often make us feel as though we've lost our hearts entirely. We long for love, but resist it at the

---

[21] 1 Cor 13:7 ESV
[22] 1 Cor 13:8

same time. Why? How can it be that we distance our hearts from the only medicine that can heal them? "The heart is deceitful above all things and beyond cure," writes the prophet Jeremiah, "who can understand it?" (Jer 17:9) This is a great mystery, but only to us. Not to God. "If our hearts condemn us, we know that God is greater than our hearts, and he knows everything" (1 John 3:20). Thus we learn from Holy Scripture that only God can navigate the hidden labyrinth of the human heart. This is a great comfort for those of us who have exerted enormous amounts of time and energy attempting to wrangle our burdened hearts. As the song says, we are forever trying to get our hearts back, but we cannot win them over ourselves; they can only be offered back to us by Love himself.

Scripture documents many powerful moments of eternal transformation in the lives of sick and suffering men and women. Over and over again we see Jesus intervening in a world of broken hearts. But life does not stop at conversion; that's when it begins. We know from the gospel record that the woman at the well was the first evangelist. After her conversation with Jesus, she returned to the village to invite her neighbors to meet him. What was her message? "Come, see a man who told me everything I ever did. Could this be the Messiah?" (John 4:29) Jesus' attention to the reality of her life convinced her of his salvific presence and became the basis for evangelism. So it is with us: "We love him because he first loved us" (1 John 4:19). In this case, Jesus' love manifested as consideration and care for the wounds of her life, but he did not leave her there. From the platform of her pain, Jesus launched Photini into a vocation of healing.

The Bible offers us a fleeting glimpse into the life of the church's first evangelist, but Photini's legacy grew over time. Later church tradition expands upon her story. The Synaxarion (a chronicle of the lives of the saints) records that first she converted her five sisters and her two sons, who all become tireless and potent evangelists of the gospel. She and her family became influential missionaries in Samaria and beyond. Her sons Photinus and Joses were martyred by Nero, and Photini, in one of the most poetic martyrdoms in Christian history, was thrown down a well to her death. A well had been her entry into salvation, and a well became her gateway into glory.

Photini's story offers the same message as the song: to the extent that we manifest Divine Love, it renews and ennobles our souls. Love overcomes the darkness of our former identities, and propels us into new life in Christ, transforming other lives in an unbroken chain from Photini and her contemporaries until now. Divine favor is of course her true reward, yet even on earth Photini's influence has never been forgotten. Because of her steadfast piety and exponential impact, the Eastern Church has awarded St. Photini the title "Equal to the Apostles." Her encounter with Jesus was so profoundly transformative that she committed the rest of her life to embodying the grace she had been given. This was the first manifestation of the evangelical tradition of the church, and it forged an enduring legacy that extends to all believers today.

In like manner, Clark's song—indeed, the entire album—is also an embodiment of divine intervening love. It is a record of a man fighting for his own heart. But it goes beyond that. Like the woman at the well, he is not content merely to hold space for his own healing; rather, he creates artifacts of grace—music, poetry, this book—that hold space for our healing. In that way, he continues in the tradition of the first evangelist, Photini, the "enlightened one," one of the first saints who teaches us—teaches me—what it means to find my heart in Divine Love.

6

The Heart of Our God

"The context of this face to face seeing has been mortally dangerous, wounding combat. Rembrandt has a painting of the scene which interprets it profoundly. In it, Jacob . . . is having his neck slowly and painfully turned so that he looks his opponent in the face. It is salvation as the terrible struggle with a God who is content with nothing less than complete reconciliation face to face. On the cross too there is a wrestling, there is a wounding to the point of death, the identity of a people and of God is at stake, and there is eventual blessing. It is as if the whole drama is a way of painfully wrenching our necks to focus on this dead face as the sign of reconciliation."
David Ford, *Self and Salvation*

"For the message of the cross is foolishness to those who are perishing, but to us who are being saved it is the power of God."
1 Cor 1:10

God knows I want to be clever.

I want to say some cute thing that will turn the tables on someone and what they've been thinking about Jesus, about his death, about sin. I want to make the cross seem a little less foolish, probably, and alleviate some of my own embarrassment as a worshipper of a humble God in this world that is obsessed with power as "winning" over against another person.

As brilliant as St. Paul is, he's pretty emphatic that when it comes to the cross, charm, persuasive power, and cleverness won't cut it. This is something incomprehensible, but comprehensive knowing is not all it's cracked up to be. Gloriously, even if we can't get our heads all the way around Jesus and his work at the cross, we can, like John leaning his head against Jesus' breast at the Last Supper, make real saving contact with the Lord. After all, Jesus didn't do what he did to give us a new "big idea," he came to give us himself. Whether we understand the cross or not, we can have *him*. If we have him, what else is there?

When I was nine years old, my parents sent me to a summer camp in the Ozark mountains. I loved it, but I was an angry child. I threw a tantrum one day, cussed out my poor counselor, and physically attacked him.

Late that night, after everyone was asleep, he walked me out to a spot in the middle of campus. We sat on the tailgate of an old red wagon under a big streetlight. There was no great explosive worship experience. No pyrotechnics or emotional rhetoric. He simply shared the gospel. He helped me identify the burden of guilt that was so frustrating to my young heart (the guilt made me angry). He told me that I didn't have to solve or carry that guilt; Jesus wanted to forgive me and I could hand it over to him.

I wept with guilt. Then I wept with relief.

Over the years that followed, I've spent time exploring the work of Jesus intellectually. It's one of the most fruitful things to think about, especially since intelligence is a practice, not a possession—a verb more than a noun. *Intelligence* means to read into the reality of things and discern God's handwriting. Again, we wind up facing a Person who is God, and we're practicing attentiveness to his real presence, like Mary who has chosen the only truly necessary thing.[23]

Jesus is not a concept to master; he's a person to love and be loved by. He saved me before I had much capacity for understanding him. He turned his face towards me, and asked me to turn my face towards him. He opened his arms and invited me, like John, to lay myself against his breast.

---

[23] Lk 10:42

The Heart of Our God

Now, I know that it's hard to talk about
I know guilt and shame and sin
And punishment and wrath are awkward at best
And at worst unmentionable things

But we can't just pretend like we all are okay
Like what's under the rug doesn't haunt us
Out of sight never did take the cancer away
And we could use some good news, if we're honest

But it's hard to look up at a man on a cross
Hard to feel the full weight of our glory
If it means that the good thing we each might have been
Went *this* wrong and now *this* is our story

That however far from his beauty we fell
That man hanging there is the hard truth
Of what God had to do to remove the disease
Of rebellion that killed all his family

'Cause I swear you weren't born with these chains on your arms
You were made to dance free as a song
It was not God's intent that your life would be spent
Slowly dying alone with no hope you could find your way home

Now, whatever you've heard about love up 'til now
And whatever they say about God
Well, I don't think you'll find a more beautiful thing
Than a friend who would lay down his life

And I promise it's worth it to stare down the worst
To face up to a Face crucified
If it means we can find an old highway has cleared
That leads home to the heart of our God

The Way Home
Matthew Clark

I cried the first time I killed a deer.

I cried little-boy tears as I laid my hand on the beautiful creature's body and felt its life leave it—because of me. I watched as blood emptied onto the grass from the hole where my bullet had pierced the doe's now unmoving chest. I prayed a prayer of sorrowing thanks for the life laid down to feed me and my family.

These days I stroll through the grocery store and pick up shrink-wrapped meats, and I can assure you that very rarely do I tenderly lay my hand on the packaging and weep. The very real death of a fellow creature feels too abstract for that. It's easy to forget that we do not generate our own life; rather, the pattern embedded throughout all of creation is that we receive our life from outside of ourselves when some living thing is emptied of life for our sake. Alexander Schmemann says:

> Man must eat in order to live; he must take the world into his body and transform it into himself, into flesh and blood. He is indeed that which he eats, and the whole world is presented as one all-embracing banquet table for man. And this image of the banquet remains throughout the whole Bible, the central image of life. It is the image of life at its creation and also the

image of life at its end and fulfillment: ". . . that you eat and drink at my table in my kingdom." . . . Man is a hungry being. But he is hungry for God. Behind all the hunger of our life is God. All desire is finally a desire for him. To be sure, man is not the only hungry being. All that exists lives only by "eating."[24]

The first time we encounter this reality is at our birth. We don't bring ourselves into this world; someone carries, feeds, and finally bleeds and suffers so that we may be here at all. And good parents will go on emptying themselves for their children's sake. But even more basic is the fact that we must breathe, eat, and drink to stay alive, and we cannot generate air, food, and drink from within ourselves; they must be received from another.

This pattern is so plain and so pervasive that it's nearly invisible; it's so obvious it's obscure. We forget one of the deepest and most constant realities of our existence: everything in the world empties itself for the sake of something else. Start looking for the pattern. And start looking for the places where the pattern breaks down; in those cases, you'll find a thousand kinds of selfishness eating away at human hearts.

In light of this pattern, when we see Jesus "*emptying himself* by taking on the form of a slave . . . [and] becoming obedient to the point of death . . . on a cross," this shouldn't strike us as particularly strange. Since the world was made through him, it makes perfect sense that he would follow the pattern that he himself embedded in his own creation. And the world was made with this self-emptying pattern at its heart because that's the pattern of life that has existed among the three Persons of the Trinity since before the world began; self-emptying love is the way of Reality itself.[25]

---

[24] Alexander Schmemann, *For the Life of the World: Sacraments and Orthodoxy*. (Crestwood, NY: St. Vladimir's Seminary Press, 2004), 11, 14.

[25] In 2 Peter 1:3, we're told that God's work of salvation enables us to become real partakers in God's divine nature. This includes being conformed to the likeness of the One who empties himself in love for others (in keeping with the life of the Trinity). Or as 1 John 3:16 says, "This is how we know what love is: Jesus Christ laid down his life for us; and we ought to lay down our lives for our brothers and sisters."

Fairy tales also testify to the common sense of the thing: dragons demand the sacrifice of a virgin and monsters want to eat innocent children. Pagan humanity intuited something of the same pattern; almost every ancient culture had some transactional system requiring death to sustain life.[26] Ancient Israel's sacrificial system emphasizes this pattern through sacrificial lambs. Blood is spilled, and people are restored to the community of God.

What is surprising about the cross—what nobody saw coming—was that God himself would *become* the lamb of God who takes away the sin of the world. That the life that would be poured out for us would be his own. Why do we need *his* life, specifically? Maybe we can make sense of it by taking simple nutrition as a clue. For instance, we eat certain foods because they provide a particular life-giving component that we need to grow, to survive an illness, or for our bodies to rebuild after an injury.

But there's no food on the planet that can supply the life-giving component we need to recover from the disease of sin or restore us to bodily life after having died. We need heavenly food, heavenly drink. John says, "This is how we know what love is: Jesus Christ laid down his life for us; and we ought to lay down our lives for our brothers and sisters" (1 John 3:16).

God has given us these patterns in the world that work on our imaginations as living metaphors. Built into the very stuff of the cosmos, they prepare our hearts and minds to perceive the reality from which they are derived. When Jesus says he is the bread of life, he's saying that all the bread we've ever eaten wasn't really bread, it was an analogy for the *real thing*: Jesus' body. When he says that he has living water, he's saying that all the water you've

---

[26] However, pagan sacrificial systems (idolatry) were an attempt to manipulate deities, whereas the Israelite "was doing what God in his mercy commanded be done. There is no hint that any magic is being applied or any attempt to coerce God. There are no pagan ideas of appeasement of an offended deity. Atonement is of divine origin and sin is put away only because God wills it and has ordained means whereby it can be accomplished. We see this in the work of Christ." Leon Morris, *The Atonement, Its Meaning and Significance* (Downers Grove, IL: Inter-Varsity Press, 1983), 86.

ever drunk has prepared you for what water really signifies: the Holy Spirit[27] whom Jesus intends to give. And this is true of everything God has made; as the poet G. M. Hopkins says so beautifully, "[Each mortal thing] acts in God's eye what in God's eye [it] is—/ Chríst—for Christ plays in ten thousand places."[28] All of creation signals towards its true self: Christ.[29]

Well, all except one thing. Sin.

We know something's not right with this world. There is something that simply doesn't belong; something has invaded and taken deep root in the world itself and in us, causing every imaginable kind of suffering.

"The depravity of man is at once the most empirically verifiable reality but at the same time the most intellectually resisted fact," quipped Malcolm Muggeridge.[30] Evil and the suffering it leads to have become so normal to us, yet we can never quite accept them as natural or right. And what about us? Honesty insists we admit that this unbelonging brokenness has infected us down to our very marrow. What a terrifying fact to face! In reply to the question "What is wrong with the world?" G. K. Chesterton stated simply, "I am."[31] He was brave enough to cease resisting "the most empirically verifiable reality" of sin.

If something that doesn't belong has taken such a thorough hold of us, it's no wonder that we can't manage to feel like we belong here, either. We can't relax. We can't be at peace. We feel haunted by grief and loss, at all times wishing we could tune out the ever-present sound of a gavel pulsing in our own veins,

---

[27] "Let the one who believes in me drink. Just as the scripture says, 'From within him will flow rivers of living water.'" (Now he said this about the Spirit, whom those who believed in him were going to receive, for the Spirit had not yet been given because Jesus was not yet glorified)" (John 7:38-39 NET).

[28] Gerard Manley Hopkins, "As Kingfishers Catch Fire," *God's Grandeur and Other Poems* (New York: Dover Publications, 1995), 36.

[29] John's Gospel introduces Jesus as the incarnation of the Word/*logos*, the living, personal origin and rationale of every created thing.

[30] Anecdotal.

[31] The precise origin of the quote in this form is debated, but most likely it grew anecdotally out of Chesterton's editorial in *The Daily News*, August 16, 1905. There his comment reads, "In one sense, and that is the eternal sense, the thing is plain. The answer to the question "What is Wrong?" is, or should be, "I am wrong." For a more in-depth exploration visit: https://www.jordanmposs.com/blog/2019/2/27/whats-wrong-chesterton

circulating thick, red guilt to every cell in our bodies. We can't shake the constant undercurrent of shame with its legion of voices, always whisper-shouting accusations at the children of God. We live on edge, huddled behind the door of our run-down, disheveled apartment expecting the Landlord's knock any minute, knowing we can't pay the rent and he has every right to evict us. We don't belong, because the problem isn't only "out there;" it's, as they say, in the blood. In mine, in yours.

Hebrews says, "Without the shedding of blood there is no forgiveness" (Heb 9:22). Remembering how only certain foods have the qualities needed for certain results, we realize animal blood can't supply the kind of life we desperately need. But Jesus is *true* bread and *true* drink from the eternal realm. His death[32] can supply the saving power—a new lifeblood, so to speak—that all the meals, medicine, and healing in the world are just hinting towards.

To receive into ourselves this Christ, who willingly empties himself out at the cross, births a supernatural transformation in us that begins now, endures through death itself, and continues endlessly on the other side of resurrection.

Somehow at the cross the disease of sin, the infection of evil in us (and the cosmos) is healed—and not by being swept under the rug or waved off carelessly. Do you really want the suffering you've experienced in this broken world to simply be dismissed or invalidated? The cross means that God takes our pain seriously, and in order to do that, he has to take seriously the evil causes of pain in this world. Out of sight, out of mind "never did take the cancer away." Anyone who's spent time in a healing process knows that our wounds are only compounded when we avoid them; they must be ingested; if we are to heal, we must turn to face the very worst about the world and ourselves. At the cross, Jesus refuses to turn his face from us, from sin, from death, from all the wickedness that ever was or will be, and

---

[32] It's worth pointing out that the *blood* of Jesus = the violent *death* of Jesus. This helps protect against "magical thinking," as if his blood were a sort of magical fluid. The blood's meaning is that Jesus' death has accomplished a comprehensive salvation. The same idea applies when we speak of "the cross."

he takes it into himself. "He himself bore our sins" in his body on the cross, so that we might die to sins and live for righteousness. "By his wounds you have been healed" (1 Peter 2:24).

The crucifixion of Jesus confronts us with the horrifying reality of both creation and humanity's devastation, and calls us to keep eye contact with it. At the same time, his crucifixion is proof that right in the midst of such a torturous mess is a face revealing the unfathomable depth of God's commitment to demonstrate his love to us—not once we got our act together—but "while we were still sinners" (Rom 5:8). And there's no good explanation, other than the fact that this is just how the LORD is: unaccountably graceful, unimaginably beautiful.

But *how* does the death of Jesus do what it does? The short answer is that nobody quite knows. Though the exact mechanics of the crucifixion aren't precisely explained, however, Scripture gives us an array of picture-words spanning the breadth of human experience, each helping us apprehend some particular aspect—not necessarily of *how* but of *what* Jesus's death accomplishes. Here are some examples of those picture-words:

> *Political*: imprisonment, ransom, victory, liberation
> *Religious*: sacrifice, suffering, self-surrender, substitution, atonement, renewal of life, acceptance, rejection, and more
> *Legal:* treaty, covenant, rights and duties, transgression of the law, restitution, guilt, punishment, satisfaction, reward, pardon, indemnification, repentance, compensation, justification, and more
> *Personal:* community, friendship, responsibility, disappointment, injury, broken faith, deceit, forgiveness, love,[33] and marriage

Now, I grew up hearing mainly from the legal category of picture-words, but no single category or word paints the whole picture.

---

[33] David Ford, *Self and Salvation: Being Transformed* (Cambridge: Cambridge University Press, 2000), 170n4.

They are mutually interdependent strands that when woven together reveal a beautifully complex salvation tapestry. I'm drawing a lot from Leon Morris. In his book *The Atonement,* he explores a handful of these scriptural picture-words that help us get a feel for what's happening at the cross. He says:

> How does the death of Jesus, so many years ago, bring salvation to all his people? The question is not easy to answer, but the language of the early Christians helps us come closer to an understanding. *We see there are many facets to the cross.* It may be seen as a paying of the price, as a bringing of enemies into a state of friendship, as an opening up of a way of access to God, and much more. These great words tell us much about the way of the cross in the sense that the cross is the means of dealing with all our sins.[34] (italics mine)

We need a multifaceted atonement, don't we? Humans are richly complex creatures, and the world God has made is vast and complex. Chesterton says that a complex lock requires a complex key, and that he found Christianity to be the only key adequate to the task.[35] Jesus' work is comprehensive, saving us in a variety of wonderful ways that braid together at the cross.

For instance, the legal picture-words express only part of the reality of salvation. It's true that at the cross Jesus is, as a condemned innocent, bearing our well-deserved punishment. So God plays by his own rules, saving us in a way that is right, which doesn't compromise his character. That's a cause for joy, because it means that God meets the demands he makes of us.

One legal picture-word, *propitiation*, means that the cross turns away God's wrath. Anger tells us that something we care about is being threatened, and so love and wrath go hand in hand. If God actually cares about us, then he must oppose any evil that threatens

---

[34] Leon Morris, *The Atonement, Its Meaning and Significance* (Downers Grove, IL: Inter-Varsity Press, 1983), 13.

[35] G. K. Chesterton, *Orthodoxy* (Project Gutenberg, 2005), chap. 6, https://www.gutenberg.org/cache/epub/130/pg130.html.

us, which means that wrath is part of the dire equation that the cross somehow solves.

To express realities that the legal terms don't, we're also given family and marriage picture-words. They tell of a Father who has found a Bride for his most beloved Son, a Bride overwhelmed by tragedy, and the Son sent to redeem her from enemies too strong for her and bring her home. For any family member who's being held hostage (whether as result of his own foolishness or outside oppression), the cross declares that God has paid the costly ransom for every loved one's safe return.

Alongside picture-words, scriptural narratives can populate our imaginations with story-shapes that offer templates for understanding God's work in the Gospels. Let's take the Exodus story. God raises up a prophet like Moses from among his own people who are in a state of oppression and slavery. Jesus, the true Moses, makes a safe pathway through the previously uncrossable sea. No human effort could have parted it, but the death of Jesus splits sin and death in half so we can pass through and rendezvous with the Father on the other side—not at the foot of untouchable Mt. Sinai, but at

> Mount Zion . . . the city of the living God, the heavenly Jerusalem. You have come to thousands upon thousands of angels in joyful assembly, to the church of the firstborn, whose names are written in heaven. You have come to God, the Judge of all, to the spirits of the righteous made perfect, to Jesus the mediator of a new covenant, and to the sprinkled blood that speaks a better word than the blood of Abel. (Heb 12:22-24)

And what about the plagues that exposed the emptiness of Egypt's gods? In a beautifully ironic move, Jesus becomes the plague *and* the plagued-one, the suffering servant who by his humility humiliates the false gods of invulnerability, coercion,

---

[36] The cross plays on the third commandment: not to make God's name appear empty or vain. Jesus takes the worldly powers' names in vain, exposing them as empty, feeble, devoid of any real power.

and status. He shows us what a real God is like, and reveals how empty[36] the things we've trusted in really are. I like how Eugene Peterson translates Colossians 2:15: "He stripped all the spiritual tyrants in the universe of their sham authority at the cross and marched them naked through the streets" (MSG). Jesus takes the idols' names in vain (because they are vain), and gives us, at the cross, the One Name that really can be trusted to save us.

Speaking of vain gods, lately I've wondered whether all of our defense mechanisms and coping strategies are really just ways that we attempt to simulate the actual atonement Jesus accomplished on the cross. For instance, blame is an effort to get our sin off ourselves and onto some scapegoat, and denial is an effort to recover innocence by pretending sin isn't there. Vulnerability is frightening, so we attempt to manufacture a sense of safety in an untrustworthy world through control; Jesus trusts his Father in the midst of human betrayal, and offers us a love willing to die rather than betray us. People-pleasing is a performance intended to buy our way into belovedness; Jesus gives that love freely, though we have no leverage. Our pain and our illicit pleasures can become means of escape, ways we numb ourselves to the despair we feel over any possibility of joyful intimacy; Jesus has won for us intimate access to every pleasure inherent in the splendor of holy love. *Legalism* describes a strategy that makes legality the qualifier of rightness; Paul debunks this approach, pointing out that just because something is legal doesn't make it right.[37] Legalism is as common today as it was in Jesus' and Paul's time; we still warp the meaning of words describing our sins and pass laws that effectively label various evils "good." These are ways we "move the target" so our terrible aim appears to be hitting the bullseye. We're merely trying to justify ourselves; Jesus accomplishes real justification, not by moving the target, but by becoming the bullseye and absorbing every errant arrow into himself.

---

[37] 1 Cor 10:23

We could keep going, but you get the idea. We intuit that we're made for a state of belovedness, peace, and joy, and that there really is some sliver of truth in all our unsuccessful attempts to recover it. We wouldn't bother with the simulations if they didn't brush up against reality at least a little bit, but now that Christ has died for us, all those human efforts are obsolete. We can let go of simulations because the Real has come.

How can we help but be captivated by our beautiful liberator? While it is fun to wonder about the love we've been shown, I'm relieved to remember that the work of Christ saves me, and not how well I understand or can explain it. Leon Morris says, "We are saved, not by some fine theory and not by some blinding revelation, and certainly not by our own best effort, but by Christ's atoning death."[38] C.S. Lewis agrees, saying:

> The central belief is that Christ's death has somehow put us right with God and given us a fresh start. Theories as to how it did this are another matter: A good many different theories have been held as to how it works; what all Christians are agreed on is that it does work. . . . A man can eat his dinner without understanding exactly how food nourishes him. A man can accept what Christ has done without knowing how it works.[39]

The glory of Yahweh's saving works can never be fully exhausted. For now, we've been given picture-words and story-shapes that allow us to touch and be touched by (apprehend) what we cannot possibly get our heads around (comprehend). We cannot drink the sea dry, yet we may joyfully plunge into the coolness of the vast baptismal blue of Living Water.

---

[38] Morris, 12.
[39] C. S. Lewis, *Mere Christianity: A Revised and Amplified Edition* (London: HarperCollins Publishers, 2002), 54–55.

In the end, Jesus' death is not merely a loving gesture that reassures us of God's affection (though it certainly is that), but a real, supernatural, and necessary work, without which there could be no hope of escape or healing from all that is wrong with the world, including all that is so deeply broken and wounded in our own hearts. Without it, there's no way home to where we belong. No way for our deepest God-given hunger to be met. But now, our Father has set a table for a wedding feast and the Groom's proposal lingers in the air, a fragrant hope blowing in on a Wind from "beyond the walls of the world."[40]

The wonders of what the Father, Son, and Holy Spirit have done through the ministry, death, and resurrection of Jesus are inexhaustible. Even angels marvel at and long to explore these things.[41] Jesus is a Word we can never finish saying, just as there is a word of perfect love that comes through his face that can never be silenced. Jesus is proof that God has indeed turned his face towards us in love and uttered an eternal "syllable of water"[42] that quenches our desperate thirst for belovedness, secures our forgiveness, and rinses us clean, that opens a new and living way through the uncrossable sea by the cross of Christ—a way home to the heart of our God.

---

[40] J. R. R. Tolkien, *Tree and Leaf: Including the Poem "Mythopoeia"* (Boston: Houghton Mifflin, 1989), 62.
[41] 1 Peter 1:12
[42] Emilie Griffin, *A Syllable of Water: Twenty Writers of Faith Reflect on Their Art* (Brewster, MA: Paraclete Press, 2008).

7

Only the Lover Sings

> "Being a singing self in the sense of
> [Ephesians] 5:18-20 is the most obvious realisation
> of an identity formed through the gospel."
> David Ford, *Self and Salvation*

> "And let us run with perseverance the race marked
> out for us, fixing our eyes on Jesus, the pioneer
> and perfecter of faith. For the joy set before him he
> endured the cross, scorning its shame, and sat down
> at the right hand of the throne of God. Consider him
> who endured such opposition from sinners, so that
> you will not grow weary and lose heart."
> Heb 12:2–3

One night, the three of us climbed through the hatch onto the dormitory rooftop and laid ourselves right near the edge. Far below, students, made small by the distance, walked from the bright circumference of one streetlight to the next, unaware of us. Little bits of tarred gravel pressed into our backs as I and my two college buddies talked into the wee hours, gazing at the stars.

We were all believers, active in ministry. Perhaps each of us, in one way or another, felt called to ministry after college. Over the previous year or so, these lingering late night conversations had happened fairly often, but this one was different. A threshold moment.

One of our company opened his heart in a way he hadn't before. He led us into some chapters of his story we'd not known about, and would not have guessed. The result was interesting to me: instead of feeling like my friend was less than who I'd thought he was, I felt like there was just more of my friend there for me to be friends with. Something of him that had been out of reach was now within reach. At hand. Touchable.

Recently, someone said they felt a piece of my writing was vulnerable, and asked how I'd managed that. I laughed and said, "Maybe I have terrible boundaries!" The truth is, I try not to share things in writing that I haven't already shared and worked through with close friends.

Of course, I often hide my true self just like everybody else. But I always come back around to the fact that my deepest desire isn't to be safe, but to be deeply known. At some point, the price of safety is too high. The difficulty of allowing my true self to show up warts and all is worth it, if it means making real contact. Real contact as opposed to bumping up against one another's facades or personas.

What a gift it has been to have friends who'll pioneer in humility: friends who go first, opening the way for me to allow myself to be known. The psalmists do this, as do the best writers: not always saying what they ought to say, but what they really feel.

Astonishingly, the greatest pioneer in vulnerability is God himself.

In the Old Testament, God expresses frustration and brokenheartedness. Beside Jacob's well, Jesus makes no pretense about his weariness. It was a memorable enough detail for John to include. He "goes first" when the Samaritan woman arrives, admitting his own neediness, asking her for help. So many times throughout the Gospels, Jesus plainly weeps, shows anger, grief, fear, joy, longing, soul exhaustion. Then, nakedness and agony on a cross.

God has shown us his true face. He's making real contact possible. If even God isn't trying to make a good impression, surely we don't have to keep up appearances. We don't have to fool ourselves anymore. We don't have to fool anybody. The big surprise is that if I meet him in that vulnerable place, there will be more of me available for Jesus to love. That makes me want to sing.

Only the Lover Sings

You've never met a liar
You've only met the lie that they put forth
There ain't no soul more lonely
Until you tell the truth you can't be touched
And I wanna be touched
I wanna be touched

Only the lover sings
Only the one who dares to
look you full-on in the face
Finds out the shocking good news

I learned a terrible habit
I speed away when the red light says to stay
And when the green light's flashing
I go to sleep to keep the light at bay

But I wanna wake up

What will you find if you look into those eyes?
It's hard to believe
but maybe you're in for a surprise

I feel a new song coming
Swinging like a blade that cuts through fear
I don't owe jack to confusion
Now love has come and made himself so clear

And I wanna trust
I wanna be touched
I wanna wake up
I wanna trust

Excavation
Jessie Todd

My great-grandfather was a miner in the foothills of southern Scotland in the early twentieth century. From my grandmother I've heard stories of the lives that men like her father led—waking early and processing down the street in the light gray of a Scottish morning, equipment in tow, ready for another grueling day of excavation. The conditions were understandably difficult but the work was honest and important. My great-grandfather, like his fellow miners, left the house each morning with the simple goal of extracting something useful from the earth.

Thinking about this process of mining, I have researched other types of mines from around the world. In South Africa, just west of Johannesburg, lies the largest gold mine in the world. There, workers extract gold encased in rubble, and then work delicately to free the gold from the rock around it. Similarly, in Madagascar, sapphire miners dig deep into the rainforest, then sift through sand and dirt in search of the precious gemstones. Watching videos about these mines, I realize that I am by no means cut out for dangerous manual labor—but I can't help but admire this type of work. There is something about the process of freeing from the depths something meant to be helpful or beautiful or adored that reminds me of grace.

> *The woman said to him, "Sir, give me this water so that I won't get thirsty and have to keep coming here to draw water."*
> *He told her, "Go, call your husband and come back."*
> *"I have no husband," she replied.*
> *Jesus said to her, "You are right when you say you have no husband. The fact is, you have had five husbands, and the man you now have is not your husband. What you have just said is quite true."* (John 4:15-18)

In the story of the woman at the well, or the Samaritan woman, we witness a woman who is very much beaten down by and encased within the world around her. Nearly every part of her life could be labeled shameful—her gender, her race, her religion, her marital status (or lack thereof). She clearly wears that shame on her shoulders—the weight of it making each step heavy, making her feel shunned and scorned. She comes to the well to draw water in the heat of the day to avoid the stares and whispers of the community who cast her out. In coming alone at an off-peak hour, she expects the solitude of isolation. What she experiences instead is a life-changing encounter with the Christ.

From the outset, we notice her shock at this unexpected interaction with Jesus, simply because she was a Samaritan woman and not used to acknowledgment from Jewish men. But Jesus, reaching out to her in spite of her rank, elevated her to the status of an equal. All over the Gospels we see Christ bestowing dignity as he interacts with the shunned of his world—whether it's to break barriers of race, of gender, of class, of ability (the blind, sick, or crippled), or of age—elevating these men and women to an equal societal class. And while any egalitarian hippie might seek to correct these societal insufficiencies, Christ does not stop at correcting the shames that were laid upon her by the world. He wants to go further than that. To dig deeper than that. Beyond desiring to raise her out of the shame that society has put upon her, he seeks to redeem even the shame and burdens she has heaped upon herself from every wrongful action and every poor decision.

When I was a child, I watched many a courtroom drama, thanks to my attorney father. In these movies, the climactic scene was often painfully formulaic: the prosecutor questions the accused, the defendant tells his fabricated alibi that threatens the prospect of a guilty verdict, the prosecutor finds a flaw in the story and brings the accused's lie crumbling to the ground. And hooray! The truth will out! The guilty party is shocked and shamed, convicted, shackled, and dramatically led away. Justice is served. As a child it felt right and satisfying to see the victim justified and the wrongful brought low.

Wanting to uncover the hidden truth about someone is natural. Even as a child it was ingrained in me. I wanted to see the right and easy end to a messy crime. Also natural: letting that labeled truth become an identity. A man who steals is a thief. A person who kills someone is a murderer. A woman who makes up a story is a liar. It's how we learn to organize our world from a young age: *this* person goes in *this* box labeled with *this* title. Perhaps it's also how we still view ourselves: I'm *this* person who's done *this* thing so I am a ____ and I belong among ____. Christ's encounter with the Samaritan woman not only questions this simplistic thinking, but threatens to destroy it.

When Jesus outs the Samaritan woman as living in sexual sin (at a time when adultery was a crime worthy of stoning in the Jewish culture), he does not have his glorious "prosecutor moment" like in the movies I grew up watching. He does not reveal that truth about her character in an effort to add to her shame—but to extricate her from it. He already raised her from her low societal ranking by acknowledging her as a person; he now raises her from the depths of her sin by calling it out and setting it aside. Going back to the climax of the courtroom scene, it's as if the prosecutor reveals that the accused was lying during his testimony—then walks over to the witness stand, rests his arms on the bench, and says, "So, how are you doing?" No jury convicts him. No wrists are shackled. Prosecutor and prosecuted might just as easily go get some coffee.

This is the image of the Christ I've come to know and love. Like my great-grandfather in Scotland, Jesus hits the streets each morning with tools for excavation in hand. He knows that there is good to be found within the depths, and he braves the mines for our sake.

And we lie buried within. Piled on and around us are the burdens of this world, this life—what we have done and what has been done to us. We lie in darkness, edges rough and split. But we can be extracted from all that encases us by the strong and steady hand of love. All we have known and accepted to be part of who we are—our sins, our shames, our traumas—can be chiseled away until the truest form of ourselves is revealed. The *us* we were made to be. Our Eden-selves.

When I picture Jesus with the woman at the well, I imagine him offering her this freedom of excavation. Of being extracted from the shames that have defined and weighed her down—but there is a moment where the decision is up to her. Because we are not inanimate stones, we are beings with a soul and a will, we are free to avert grace's chisel and remain embedded within our shames. It's tempting to stay hidden. To "speed away when the red light says to stay," as Matthew Clark says in his song "Only the Lover Sings." Why, when offered an out, do many of us remain impacted within the rubble that holds us down?

There are probably many reasons we hide, but I think they have to do with trust and not wanting to be seen. A quote from pastor

Tim Keller's book *The Meaning of Marriage* has helped me understand this fear. He writes, "To be loved but not known is comforting but superficial. To be known and not loved is our greatest fear. But to be fully known and truly loved is, well, a lot like being loved by God. It is what we need more than anything. It liberates us from pretense, humbles us out of our self-righteousness, and fortifies us for any difficulty life can throw at us."[43] This idea of being unconditionally loved by someone is an ideal for relationships, but one we rarely see demonstrated to us. I have been lucky to witness a few beautiful marriages in which each spouse creates a safe space for the other to be vulnerable, to grow, and to be honest. Perhaps there can be no real intimacy without the belief that we will not be shamed for our faults or issues or trauma. Without witnessing a love like this, it's natural to doubt it could ever be found—even in the Lord.

I remember as a kid walking back from the park one night with my dad. I don't know what inspired our conversation, but we were going back and forth playing a "Would you still love me if ___?" game. I remember asking things like, "If I said a mean word, would you still love me?" to which my dad would respond, "I'd still love you." I remember asking the worst thing I could think of: "If I broke your computer, would you still love me?" He paused and said, "I'd probably be really mad . . . but I'd still love you." Since that conversation, I've said a lot of mean words, and while I haven't broken a computer, I have broken and been broken. Thankfully, I've had a father who has loved me still, giving me a foundational knowledge of unconditional love.

I don't know if the Samaritan woman had witnessed this type of love from a husband, a father, or a friend—but I do know that she trusted this stranger-prophet-man enough to let him chisel her

---

[43] Timothy Keller with Kathy Keller, *The Meaning of Marriage: Facing the Complexities of Commitment with the Wisdom of God* (New York: Penguin Books, 2011), 101.

out of her shame. What I see in this story is true, unconditional love—a love that looks her in the eye and gives a new identity. By daring to meet the gaze of the man who already saw her—all that had piled upon her and all that she was—she was able to see herself differently. To see herself as he saw her. As whole. As Daughter. She was no longer the low-ranking sinner at the well. She was simply who she was. Her burdens lifted, she ran into the village that had shunned her and told them of the man who excavated her from the rubble of her life. "Could this be the Messiah?" (John 4:29)

This mission to break apart and free the gold and gems embedded within the bedrock of the world is the restoration Jesus sought to bring us when he came to earth. When we pray for his kingdom to come down, we are not praying for some holy, immaculate city to fall from the sky and replace this planet. We are praying for Jesus to chisel away more of what has hidden the jewels that are already here. We are praying to be instruments of excavation. We are praying for the strength to be broken out of our own sediment. Like the woman at the well—this saint at the well—that restoration and acceptance allows us to run freely, shoulders light, into a hurtful world, declaring with each step that grace has touched this body and this soul. With delicate hands, my dirt has been removed. I've been seen truly—for my shames and my scars and my sins—and I am unconditionally loved.

8

The Return of the Prodigal Son

"We live our lives on the brink of a great beginning."
Amy Baik Lee, "The Bright Window"

"Surely your goodness and love will follow me all the days of my life, and I will dwell in the house of the Lord forever."
Ps 23:6

There are some incredibly awkward things that are absolutely worth doing.

A bunch of us milled around the room while someone poured water into the basins. The retreat leader had given simple instructions, and we were getting ready to try a little exercise in blessing. We would receive a blessing and we'd have a chance to offer it to another: a little dab of water from the basin to help get us inside the story of Jesus' baptism at the Jordan, then hands on shoulders, eye contact, and these words: *You* are my beloved son; in you I am well-pleased.[44]

God the Father's words to his son. Ratifying words. Locating words. Life-giving words.

It is good to have a reliable parent. It's wonderful to be provided for. But there is something about being received with joy, celebrated, trusted, delighted in. No doubt a child has practical needs: food, clothing, shelter. But notice what God the Father doesn't say. He doesn't say here, "You are my son; I'll make sure you have the stuff you need."

A few years ago, after playing a concert, I found a little card someone had left for me. I don't know who, but they'd written the Father's words: "You *are* my son; in you I am well-pleased." I've kept it on my desk ever since, because I can't survive without the reminder. Just like the need to say the post-communion prayer every week:

> Almighty and everliving God,
> we thank you for feeding us with the spiritual food
> of the most precious Body and Blood
> of your Son our Savior Jesus Christ;
> and for assuring us in these holy mysteries
> that we *are* living members of the Body of your Son,
> and heirs of your eternal kingdom.

When we wander off and find ourselves in a foreign country, dislocated. When we're robed in sad names that stain us like the muck of the pigsty. Whether we're our own worst enemy, under the heel of an external enemy, or just caught up in the general entropy of this fallen and ever-falling world, we need this declaration to situate us in a correspondence of love with our Heavenly Father, ratify us as his, and offer the astonishing assurance that we are even—can you believe this?—*enjoyed*.

A thousand times I've heard those words. They beckon me from the distance until I can believe again that I do have a home and a family to turn back to. Threshold words, repeated, ever urging us across the bright brink to another new beginning, and another, and another. Mercy never ceasing.

---

[44] Matt 3:17

The Return of the Prodigal Son

I am aching, brother, aching for someplace to lay my head
I am searching, darling, searching for a bit of daily bread
Well, I thought I heard you speaking, thought I felt you drawing near
Like the touch of some old memory that I wait for year to year

Oh, this is the return of the prodigal son

Oh, and still I keep that picture somewhere in the back of my mind
With your hands upon my shoulders, where you held me in a holy light
Someone said we live our lives on the brink of a great beginning
I'm still praying for that miracle—some glimpse of a happy ending

A fool can hope someone could be
Fool enough to show him mercy
To love this dead man back to life

Learning to Walk Again
Adam R. Nettesheim

A Child's First Steps

Recovery is not always a smooth, level path. We can falter or stumble into an alley or a side street that takes us the long way 'round or that winds up in a dead end, a place where we must again find our way back to that old road. The force that pulls us towards redemption, the Love at the center of life itself, can and will lead us home. But our journey starts by putting one foot in front of the other.

What might we expect those first steps to be?

Perhaps we can gain some perspective by remembering our first physical steps. Was your first attempt at walking on chubby little toddler legs a success? Did you immediately go striding across the room with a smirk on your lips while executing the occasional handspring just because you could? If you're like most of humanity, the first steps you took probably looked far less . . . successful.

Chances are you had tried to stand up many times before and couldn't. When you finally did rise, you wobbled like a hippopotamus on roller-skates. Likely you held vertical for a second, wavered, shook, and staggered . . . and then fell back on your diapered backside. Did shame and doubt stop you from ever trying again? Not likely: this was back when trying new things and failing was a way of life. You weren't yet burdened with the need to perfect every first attempt. Your self esteem had yet to buckle under the weight of initial ineptitude.

Like heroes of old, you and your valiant tender feet did not languish forever. Again and again, you would rise anew . . . only to wibble and wobble and fall over. But every time you learned what didn't work, and your legs got stronger with each attempt. And ultimately, your caregivers' acceptance and encouragement helped you learn, through much trial and error . . . to walk. Whether out of tenacious exuberance, a need to be held by the loving arms extended to you, or pulled by the miraculous force that leads us further up and further in, you took your first steps.

Look at you go! Oh! You can do it! Keep coming! I'm right here! Just look at me!

But these would not be our only first steps. Anything newly attempted carries that wibbly-wobbly feeling of our chubby toddler toes in our first Neil Armstrong-esque footfall on the carpet. But beginnings can also be difficult because most anything attempted carries with it the possibility of failure. And even long afterward, a pang of disappointment, regret, or disillusionment can throb suddenly, just like old bodily injuries do.

The way to stop all that discomfort is clear: don't try things. Or maybe try once, but certainly not twice, because failure wakes the internal magistrate who glowers and sneers and bangs its gavel, proclaiming "GUILTY OF DEFICIENCY! GUILTY OF VULNERABILITY! GUILTY OF BEING A FOOL!" But if you risk being found in contempt of that critic's court, if you risk looking comical to others, know that the adoring eyes of a Heavenly Father watch your progress. No step you take towards him, large or small, escapes his delight. He sings into every fiber of your being, giving you just enough courage to try that next step. His love is a balm for the aches that flare up with the memories of past failures.

To try, to stand, to fail, to try again and again and again, and then to do . . . it's hard. It's a big deal. And he is proud of you.

Look at you go! Oh! You can do it! Keep coming! I'm right here! Just look at me!

A Prodigal's First Steps

What about those steps that are not first attempts? What of repentances and returning back home when you've wandered off? What of restoring relationships you've neglected, tending to wounds you've inflicted? What about when apologies and amends are necessary? What if no word or deed will ever mend the broken bonds, but your spirit compels you to seek some form of restitution? In your uncertainty, difficulty, and the wibble-wobble of your first steps towards reconciliation . . . can the pleasure of the Father really be the same? Jesus speaks to this in a parable found in Luke 15.

We know that once the prodigal son makes that long journey back and plants his feet on the estate once more, his father welcomes him with open arms. But imagine for a moment that before the son makes the decision to return, the father could stand on his front porch and look through a telescope into that far-off country. Imagine he could see his son feeding pigs, covered in their filth, malnourished, ragged, scarred, and ravaged by scarcity and sin. Would his arms spread just as wide?

Or what about after the decision to return was made, but the son's first steps towards home are clearly wibbly-wobbly? A wibble for every mixed motive, a wobble for every survival instinct that inspired contrition, a stumble for every resentment that coated his regret . . . Would the father scoff and say, "Ha! Let's see if you make it this far"? Would he chuckle at every stumble or shout curses every time his son stalled a little outside a brothel or a bar before redoubling his resolve to continue on? Would he resent his son for the struggle it took to step forward with his legs and limp forward in his spirit towards home?

Human parents do not love flawlessly. But if this story is a parable about the perfect, unconditional love of God, is it not fair to say that the father who welcomed his son at the end of the road would celebrate the first steps his son took at its beginning too? Isn't it likely that this father would also pump his fist every time he saw his son overcoming an obstacle? For every time his child thought about turning back and didn't, wouldn't this father yell "That's my boy!"? This father was with him when he learned to walk the first time—not resenting any of his stumbles then, but celebrating each step towards him. This is the same father who reaches for him now as he learns to walk towards him again.

Look at you go! Oh! You can do it! Keep coming! I'm right here! Just look at me!

Are We There Yet?

As sons and daughters of our Heavenly Father, we're all still walking the road back home: each of us in different places, with different packs on our backs, different obstacles, strengths and weaknesses, scars, different reasons we ran, and different reasons for our return. Even if salvation happens in one moment, conversion takes a lifetime. And while we are still "a long way off," our Father sees us and calls us to come. Sometimes his invitations seem drowned out by the tape of our transgressions playing ever louder in our ears. We stumble, we sink, we get lost again . . . and in our darkest moments, we wonder whether the porch light is still lit.

Anyone who takes an extended car trip knows that long stretches of highway offer invitations to ask the big question: "Why?" And the more time we spend on the road back home, the more we must reckon with our reasons for going back. The danger in asking "Why?" is that we might not always like what we find.

What were the motives behind the prodigal's return? Notice what he plans to say to his father, compared to what he actually says:

> When he came to his senses, he said, "How many of my father's hired servants have food to spare, and here I am starving to death! I will set out and go back to my father and say to him: 'Father, I have sinned against heaven and against you. I am no longer worthy to be called your son; make me like one of your hired servants.'" So he got up and went to his father. . . .
> The son said to him, "Father, I have sinned against heaven and against you. I am no longer worthy to be called your son." (Luke 15:17-21)

In his moment of remorse, the prodigal's primary focus is his own destitution. He bellyaches about how well fed his father's servants are compared to his current condition, and with this as motivation, he begins to prepare an apology. This apology may invite us to ask how much of his rehearsed speech is contrition and how much is calculation. Is he crafting his speech this way because he knows which of the old man's heartstrings to pull? Because even as he crafts a humble admission of guilt and acknowledgment of the pain he caused, even as he asserts that to be disowned is just, his plea is primarily a request for some small mercy that would allow him to eat and sleep and . . . survive.

Survival is a strong motivator. If scarcity is what drove the prodigal towards home, we may wonder whether he was still focused on his father's stuff rather than on his father. Would he have wanted to return if everything was the same, but the father wasn't there? In taking his inheritance early, the prodigal essentially said that he wanted to live like his father was already dead, that to this son, Dad's stuff mattered more than Dad did. Did that really change at the end of the story or was he just going back to a place where he could get a hot meal, a bed, and a roof between him and the blistering sun?

This invites an uncomfortable moment of self-reflection. How is my journey towards my Heavenly Father like the prodigal son's to his? Is my religion more about avoiding the dangerous places I've been or the place I'm afraid the trajectory of my choices is leading me to? Am I more interested in "Dad" or in "Dad's stuff"? What about "home" captures my imagination more: getting to a place beyond the perils and pains of mortality and entering a paradise of bliss and abundance . . . or being with my Heavenly Father for eternity?

And what about my own "apologies"? Do I find myself telling God what I think he wants to hear? And even when I contritely accepted God's judgment on most things, are there a few sins I refuse to fully own up to, or some aspect of conviction I still try to deflect? Based on how defensive I get when God gets specific, I'm certainly much more comfortable accepting theoretical or categorical failings.

This personal examination can initiate a spiral of even more shame and self-incrimination. And yet, just as for the son, there is grace for us all in that ever-continuing, ever-painful journey of letting God tear off our self-protective dragon scales so we might lay all that we are, naked and vulnerable, at his feet. This story compels us to admit our own mixed motives, our incomplete and qualified confessions. And yet as much as this parable calls us to repentance, it also shows us how God's patient, loving grace is present, even in our poor power to fully, truly, deeply, and sufficiently repent.

Look at you go! Oh! You can do it! Keep coming! I'm right here! Just look at me!

There and Back Again

After a treacherous journey of legs, heart, and soul, the prodigal son rounds the corner and finds his feet on the street where he grew up. He sees the same old mailbox by the driveway, and he runs his hand along the busted fence beam that he was supposed to fix the day he decided to leave. He steps across the property line and feels a chill at the point of no return. The dogs are barking and he can see a dot on the hill that's probably his older brother, working away like he always does. If Dad was on the porch, he'd see his son by now. But when the son raises his eyes to the front porch . . . he sees it empty. His father isn't there. The porch is empty because his father has leapt off it, and is running as fast as his old legs can carry him towards the son who ran away and squandered half his hard-earned wealth.

Expecting to be battered, berated, and run off, the son closes his eyes and awaits his fate. But the father's arms do not shove or strike, nor does his mouth curse or spit. He wraps his son in a tight hug and kisses him again and again and again. Bewildered and discombobulated, the son doesn't know whether the old man has lost his mind or maybe his own mind's been affected by all that time smelling pig poo. The son finally remembers the speech he's prepared and begins it just as rehearsed. But mid-recitation, the father cuts him off.

It's not the son's speech, or the perfection of his contrition, that brings the welcome. It's the love the father has for his child. Before his "I'm sorry, Dad" can be said, his father is already calling for his servants to bring physical manifestations of sonship. The prodigal son is home.

Restored, renewed, and redeemed, the son now dances on the same floor where he learned to walk. The blistered bloody feet have been washed, anointed, and covered in beautiful shoes that stride back and forth, possibly launching him into the occasional handspring, just because he can. His mouth, once full of curses and then rehearsed apologies, can now speak forth love, praise, and gratitude to his father. Lips that once kissed so many that did not belong to him, now kiss and are kissed by those who belong to him again. His stomach, once full of the best wine and meat that his father's money could buy, then emptied of all but a stolen bite of pig slop, is now satisfied with the comfort food of the family table. His hands that once spent his father's money freely on things his dad would warn him against, and then carried slop buckets and dung shovels, are now hands washed clean and adorned with a ring of status and belonging. The shoulders that once carried off half his dad's hard-earned wealth, then drooped with shame and swine scat, are now draped in his father's best robe, the robe his father wore all those years ago with strong arms extended to that little boy learning to walk, beckoning his son to keep trying, keep getting up, keep coming towards him. And each time his boy would walk back towards him, his father was there to wrap him in his arms.

I'm Right Here Too

In some ways, every step is a first step. At each new stage of life, at each new challenge laid before us, we will need to learn again to walk towards the Father. None of us have lived this exact moment, at this exact point in history, with our exact burdens, in our exact bodies, at our exact age before. We do well to give everyone around us the grace that we need in that wibble-wobble, and we do well to see and receive the grace and love that our Heavenly Father has given us too.

God has not left us, even if we have wandered far from him. Whatever we face, whatever we've done, whatever we're afraid we cannot undo, however far we are, whether we're languishing miles and miles away, or just sulking out in the back yard, he is there, right there. He's waiting for us to turn around so he can help us take those next first steps. We will wibble, we will wobble, we will get lost and we will need to be found. But his love is greater still. His hands extend towards us, beckoning us home, wrapping us again in his embrace.

> *Look at you go.*
> *You can do it.*
> *Keep coming.*
> *I'm right here.*
> *Just look at me.*

9

I See a Light

*"Long my imprisoned spirit lay
Fast bound in sin and nature's night;
Thine eye diffused a quickening ray,
I woke, the dungeon flamed with light;
My chains fell off, my heart was free,
I rose, went forth, and followed Thee."*
Charles Wesley

*"The whole earth is filled with awe at your wonders;
where morning dawns, where evening fades,
you call forth songs of joy."*
Ps 65:8

Dad went into the army after college. Before that, he'd grown up on a little farm in rural Mississippi with pre-dawn chores to do. Mom grew up all of fifteen minutes away in another small town; her father was a woodworker and ran a cabinetry business.

As a child, I learned to tell the difference between the sound of Mom's footsteps coming down the hall in the morning to wake me, and Dad's. My parents had very different wake-up procedures. Dad's was all army and farm: he'd immediately flip the light switch, bark loud orders, and yank the sheets off. Mom's approach was decidedly more genteel: she'd tiptoe in, leaving the lights off, sit beside me on the bed, and, softly shaking my shoulder, tell me it was time to get up.

As an adult, I do not own an alarm clock; my phone sleeps at the other end of the house. I'm a very slow waker-upper. But I don't close the shades on my bedroom window, because I love the gradual approach of dawn as the early light silently pours in to fill the room. I can't help but wonder if God crafted the gentle arrival of dawn (and dusk) to bear witness to his own preferred style of approach. Jesus' first advent in Bethlehem was like that, and for those who rest in him, his second advent may not seem so startlingly sudden as it will to those who are drunk on darkness. Dawn is a headache to the hung-over.

For the prodigal son, like the Samaritan woman, every step towards the moment of waking was hard. Long night stumblings beneath the shadows of darkness. Light would be a threat; it would mean exposure. We were created naked and unashamed; we long to wind up there, but who can face the possibility of essential rejection? The explosion of light, our coverings violently yanked off. Naked and shamed.

Isn't it curious, then, that Jesus is described as a groom approaching his beloved bride? A groom who lovingly coaxes his frightened dove out from her hiding place in the cleft?[45] A groom who, as he prepares a place for us, has patiently offered a long betrothal season (too long, it feels like!), so we might acclimate by way of the slow approach of that level of intimate exposure that would otherwise be too overwhelming?

Here is a groom who washes us with water through the word. Who tenderly feeds, nourishes, and cares for his beloved. Who, when he does pull back the coverings, does so gently like the slow approach of dawn. I wonder whether what will suddenly startle us is not in the dawn, but finding the clothes that fall from us upon meeting the groom to be the ragged shadow-garments of shame. Good riddance.

The bright garment of his gaze will be our new and only adornment, clothing us in purity, for to the Pure One all things are pure.

---

[45] Song of Songs 2:14

I See a Light

I see a light, I see a light
Like a spear thrust through gloom
I hear a voice, I hear a voice
Like a song in the middle of the field of war

I see a table, I see a table
Set for the hungry in their time of need
I feel a touch, a gentle touch
Brush like a breeze in the desert heat

With all my strength I turned my face
And found you were facing me, facing me
You saw me naked there when my shame
fell 'round my feet, fell 'round my feet

I hear a song, I hear a song
Kindled in my stricken heart
I learned a dance, I learned a dance
And a music I'd not known to look for

I nearly gave up, I nearly gave up
So great the flood of evil that arose
But then the tide turned and I heard laughter
The Only Unconfused One comes to judge

The Sound of Eucatastrophe
Amy Baik Lee

"Every wink of an eye some new grace will be born."
Shakespeare, *The Winter's Tale*

The statue is exquisitely carved, the perfect likeness of his late wife.

Beholding it for the first time, the aged king is momentarily robbed of speech. He was prepared to see her figure and face, he thought, but he knows now that he wasn't prepared for all that her form would awake in him. Here, in lines far clearer than his grieving memory has been able to draw over sixteen years, are her honest eyes, her hands, her unmistakable posture of tenderness.

He sees that the sculptor has taken into account the elapsed years and shaped this image as she would have appeared now—a kindness, surely, but one that cuts as much as it comforts. For she herself would be here today if not for his suspicious rage. His groundless jealousy.

The very position of the statue reminds him of the day she was hauled, at his merciless command, out of bed after giving birth. Shame sears him as he remembers: *he made her stand trial for adultery*. On that oppressive day she still had life in her body; resolute in her innocence, though weak in her limbs, she was flushed with the warmth of a queen's breath and blood.

The coldness of this stone reproaches him, and rightly so.

The king stands still before the statue, weighted by his past iniquities: he spurned his longtime friend, who was as blameless as his wife in the matter of the imagined affair; he terrified his little son, who died of fear during the trial; he brought about the death of his wife, who collapsed and succumbed to her grief. Even his newborn daughter was banished to die by exposure to the elements.

At this moment, the audience of Shakespeare's *The Winter's Tale*—if they are familiar with the source material for this play—knows what ought to come next for King Leontes. Robert Greene wove the original threads of this plot in his 1588 prose romance *Pandosto,* and in that work the king ultimately takes his own life. Perhaps it's best to let Leontes have his moment of remorse, then; his just deserts will arrive soon enough.

But in this play, as he lingers, the hostess and owner of the statue steps forward. "If you can behold it," Paulina offers, "I'll make the statue move indeed, descend, / And take you by the hand."[46] Leontes agrees, still gazing; whatever she is able to do, he is willing to witness.

She bids the statue move.

Slowly, it descends from its pedestal. Its hand is impossibly raised, its arm extended toward the stunned king. A deep cry catches in Leontes's throat as he reaches out and the iron knot of sixteen years' sorrow begins to unravel:

"O, she's warm!"[47]

This is the *coup de théâtre* at its finest, and one of the most poignant moments in Shakespearean drama. Prior to this scene, King Leontes has already found that the daughter he disowned at birth is alive, and he has welcomed and embraced her return. Together

---

[46] Shakespeare, *The Winter's Tale,* 5.3.87-89.
[47] Shakespeare, 5.3.109.

they visit the home of a noblewoman so that the daughter might see a much-acclaimed statue of her mother. There, Leontes finds the "statue" to be no immovable sculpture but his beloved wife in living flesh, hidden away for sixteen years until the right moment.

Another word for this development is J. R. R. Tolkien's *eucatastrophe*. Tolkien defines the term within the context of fairy-stories, but it may apply to other tales as well: "it can give to child or man that hears it, when the 'turn' comes, a catch of the breath, a beat and lifting of the heart, near to (or indeed accompanied by) tears, as keen as that given by any form of literary art, and having a peculiar quality."[48] For Tolkien, eucatastrophe is not merely an unexpected turn toward a happy ending; it must also strike with a "piercing glimpse of joy"[49] that carries intimations of a reality that "denies . . . universal final defeat."[50] Leontes's exclamation is both gladsome and heartbreaking to witness because it presents us—vividly—with the fulfillment of a hope that every grieving soul has imagined and precious few have experienced within the bounds of this world: he is reunited with a long-lost loved one. When his eucatastrophe arrives, it comes to both the character and the audience like the swift surprise of a brilliant spark flaring out of unrelenting darkness.

But in order for this kind of joyous breaking-in to occur in any story, Tolkien reminds us, *dyscatastrophe* must be a true possibility.[51] A eucatastrophe is startling because the situation it enters points to the likelihood of sorrow and failure. As mortals in a fallen world, we feel the weight of this tension in such scenes as Théoden's ride from Helm's Deep in *The Two Towers*, Tirian's desperate stand before the stable door in *The Last Battle*, and Time's interlude that leaves Leontes frozen in grief at the midpoint of *The Winter's Tale*.

---

[48] J. R. R. Tolkien, "On Fairy-Stories," *Tree and Leaf* (London: HarperCollins, 2001), 69.
[49] Tolkien, 70.
[50] Tolkien, 69.
[51] Tolkien, 69.

We also see dyscatastrophe—breathe it, bear it—on a far more intimate scale in our daily lives, in the hours that threaten to swallow us up and crush all hope. The loss of a job. A terminal diagnosis. The deafening vacuum of depression. The ricocheting consequences of sin and the finality of death. How weary we are, some days—how pressed between the walls of a world that suggests, repeatedly, that our only possible responses to our brokenness are denial or despair.

Yet it was precisely to this world that unparalleled eucatastrophe came. "The Birth of Christ is the eucatastrophe of Man's history,"[52] Tolkien wrote: an event even more startling than the divine command that wrought beauty and order out of the void at the dawn of the world. Jesus came into a wrecked world. The coming of the Word of God to us was an unexpected flash in gloom, a song soaring above a battlefield, a table spread for guests of no means, a cool wind in the desert. At the hinge of our history we now "see a light"—but not because we have chosen to see by some feeble flicker of optimism. A power far greater is at work: One who keeps, authors, and delights in eucatastrophe.

To Tolkien, the Incarnation was the eucatastrophe of history, and the Resurrection was the eucatastrophe of the Incarnation. If we follow his gaze and look more closely, were there not also smaller eucatastrophes strewn along the entire road between Cana and Calvary? The woman at the well radiates astonishment at being seen and known when she tells the townspeople, "Come, see a man who told me everything I ever did" (John 4:29). Jairus's daughter rises. Bartimaeus sees. Mary Magdalene breathes freely again. Every act of healing, every resurrection, every forgotten face looked upon with compassion: these were eucatastrophes for each person who encountered Jesus.

---

[52] Tolkien, 72.

And these were merely the beginning. The story of the early church was punctuated by astounding turns that changed its trajectory. Light "like a spear thrust through the gloom" and a voice as unmistakable as "a song in the middle of the field of war" came upon Saul on the road to Damascus. Peter, feeling famished, watched a great sheet descend from the heavens, signaling a table set for even the Gentiles "in their time of need." Philip blew "like a breeze in the desert heat" into the Ethiopian eunuch's life to explain the prophecies of Isaiah—and then departed in the same manner. Like jewel-hued panes joined together in a stained-glass image, these instances show the church rising to her feet, in spite of the faithlessness and the limitations of the humans involved. Over and over, we see the continual fruition of Christ's decision to actively love his Bride and to walk with her step by step "to the very end of the age" (Matt 28:20).

This is the love that changes our day-to-day lives. When I walked through one particularly long valley of post-traumatic anxiety, my greatest surprise was finding that the presence of the Redeemer-King is as true and full at the personal level as it is at the ecclesiastical one. During that time, I began to call him my wild card—the one factor that I could neither predict nor discount in the paralysis of fear that my life had become. He simply kept showing up in unexpected places. I ran into a friend at the bookstore who asked me a question I needed to ponder. My sponsored child wrote a letter of encouragement to *me*, out of the blue and perfectly timed, to say we should "keep going with God." The daughter of a former teacher shared her story about mental illness on social media, ending with the words, "It gets better." My lungs kept drawing air and my heart kept beating even when I felt there was no earthly reason why they should, and in all of these details and a hundred more, the goodness of God kept appearing with a directness I couldn't avoid.

Through that time, I learned that his stance towards us is the reason that individuals have been able to walk through the valley of the shadow of death without fearing evil, and the reason why all his disciples are permitted—no, *instructed*—to ask him for daily sustenance. He himself is the reason we may expect a breakthrough of help and of joy in the most unlikely places.

In L. M. Montgomery's *Rilla of Ingleside,* a motherless baby suddenly cries in a darkened room on a January night. Rilla, the baby's caregiver during the tumultuous years of World War I, considers leaving him alone at first; she knows that Jims is well fed and warm. But her imagination persists in putting her in Jims's lonely place, and when she goes to pick him up—he *laughs*. He laughs for the very first time, "a real, gurgly, chuckly, delighted, delightful laugh."[53] The tiny boy has found he is not alone, and laughter is the best and most natural response to the love that lifts him, holds him, covers him.

King David knew this sensation well. "Because you are my help," he says to the Lord, "I sing in the shadow of your wings" (Ps 63:7). Even in the wilderness of our afflictions, there is space for song, because every time we draw near to him, we find the very Maker of the universe drawing near to us.[54] His steadfast favor makes all the difference in the world. The Light of the World is *for* us; the Bread of Life is broken to feed us; the breath of the Spirit is sent to give us life. If he has given us his son, "how will he not also, along with him, graciously give us all things?" (Romans 8:32). He himself has promised that every tragedy we endure will be transformed in his hand.[55]

Eucatastrophe is therefore, of all words, one of the most succinct and fitting descriptions for the experience of learning to love and be loved by Christ. Daily we come to him, making our pleas

---

[53] L. M. Montgomery, *Rilla of Ingleside* (London: Puffin Classics, 1993), 113.
[54] James 4:8
[55] Romans 8:28

known, laying down the burdens we dare to shed. In our most lucid moments, we know what we deserve. We know he sees the selfish maneuvers we have made and the commitments we have quietly neglected, the anxieties we clench behind our backs, and the pedestals we carry in hopes of being elevated and seen. But when these things shatter in our hands and we stand blighted in the aftermath, ready for condemnation, our empty palms are met with a steady touch, and we discover: *O, he's warm!*

Warm, not merely in the fact of his aliveness where once we believed him to be inaccessible or dead, but *warm* in his demeanor and his dealings with us, as only One who is deeply intent to love can be. He has come to make us whole, and—far beyond what Shakespeare could do for Leontes—to restore the years the locusts have eaten. He will not allow anything on earth or out of the earth to separate us from him.

Astonishment thus roams the stage of our own world, visiting tired and grieving souls. We who are at work in a shadowed world can still raise our heads at every reverberation of mercy, every fresh whisper of grace, for a song of life has been kindled in our hearts; he will not let it go out. And deep in the close darkness of our world, the sounds of a stirring kingdom-anthem ring out from hidden lives touched by eucatastrophe: the music of unfettered, unashamed laughter at the approach of perfect Love.

10

That Won't Stop Him

"With its embrace of the God who entered history and became a subject within it, Christianity transformed the possibilities of thought and revolutionized late antiquity's view of history. The uniqueness of the life, death, and resurrection of Jesus will never be repeated and will leave nothing unchanged. That means history is no longer an endless cycle but a singular story in which events unfold and new realities emerge."
Roger Lundin, *Beginning with the Word*

"I am worn out calling for help;
my throat is parched.
My eyes fail,
looking for my God."
Ps 69:3

In my periphery, aquamarine flashed like sky-light glancing off some castaway bottle on the ocean. This drew my eyes down through the black grid of the patio table to the concrete below. There, a square blue note was stuck to the ground. With my coffee in one hand, I stooped to read the thin handwriting. All it said was "Another lonely day."

Years ago, I was in the checkout line at 3 a.m. The young girl running the register couldn't have been twenty. She was very pregnant. It took no especially sensitive powers of observation on my part to see that she was worn out. Crossing the oily asphalt parking lot afterwards, I wondered how she got there. How would she fare from here?

It can happen like that. We can wind up in unimaginably painful places. Places we never saw coming. It's happened to me, too. I've seen it among my friends, in my family, and in the world: illness, injustice, divorce, estrangement, cruelty, apathy—a thousand thousand species of death.

This morning, I was reading Psalm 23: "The LORD is my shepherd." What kind of shepherd is he?

Is he the kind of shepherd who knows the right paths? Mapped the terrain? He is.

When we wind up in a valley surrounded by death, is he the kind of shepherd who bails? No, he's not. Nothing intimidates him; he'll go absolutely anywhere for love of the sheep, even into death itself.

What about when our enemies show up in full force to destroy us? Will he—*can* he do anything about it? Yes, and yes.

Will he get bored or frustrated with shepherding us? Never. Is he reliable? He is. All the days of our lives and then some.

Does he actually know what he's doing? Where he's going? Yes. He knows how to get us home, no matter what. No matter what life throws at us, Jesus will go there with us, face it, and keep us on the right path—the one that ends in joy.

I've been in some places that I thought I'd never get out of. Or I thought that if I ever did get out of them, I'd never get over them. And I've been surprised. I've put my weight on things that turned out to be trap doors, and I've fallen fast and had the breath knocked out of me. In the midst of my dismay and the whirling hurricane of my own confusion, I've been surprised to find Jesus, the only unconfused one, calmly taking it all in, and with his clear-eyed, holy imagination, crafting a way through it to healing and joy. As if every door locked in deadly terror were a mere curtain of mist for him to pass through and whisper, "Peace be with you."

That Won't Stop Him

Buried in a drawer like a pinewood box
There's a ring that used to shine like a promise
But it doesn't anymore

Or at the coffee place, I found a little note
It said, "Another lonely day," like a message
From a stranded castaway

It can happen like that to any one of us
Life just ain't what you thought it was

But that won't stop him, that won't stop him
from making new life, from making new life

I hear the whispers now, all with a tongue so sharp
They can fill you full of holes if you let them
Leave you paralyzed with doubt

There's so many ways that we can go so wrong
Every one of us is broken and bleeding
Too ashamed to show our face

Jesus, you are here, you're right here
In the middle of death.
But that never stopped you,
never stopped you before

All You Have to Do Is Die:
The Power of Abiding in Death
Junius Johnson

"If I go up to the heavens, you are there;
if I make my bed in the depths, you are there."
Ps 139:8

We really see the world from the inside out.

I behave and misbehave in this world on the basis of my longings, and my actions have something frantic about them. Knowing that my life in this world will not last forever, insufficiently trusting that my hope is not only for this world,[56] and fearing to miss out on things I want to see or do: these add a nervous energy to all of my actions. But this freneticism stems from my urgent need to prove that I exist, and that I am as I think myself to be: noble, true, faithful, strong, cunning, and more. And yet all my acting in the world (the behaving and the misbehaving) is fundamentally ineffectual, for I am dead in my sins. This lack of agency does not, sadly, render me entirely impotent: I am still able to affect the world, and therefore to do much harm. But my actions do not attain the end I desire, and I find myself shut out from my hopes and dreams.

Michael Ende writes, "It seems strange that we can't just wish

---
[56] 1 Cor 15:9

what we please. Where do our wishes come from? What is a wish, anyway?"[57] Because wishes express ways we want ourselves or the world to change, they reveal what we don't like about ourselves or our situation, ultimately exposing our insecurities. They therefore have great power, but an uncontrollable power. I long to take charge of these dreams, to make the world just the way I want it to be, and to acquire from others the things I want. I desire to be loved by others, to be held in high esteem, desired, and cherished, and I long for luxury: to live in wealth and abundance, to be free to sample the best that the material world has to offer.

The problem is that I pursue these desires in a destructive fashion. I approach all things in the world as if they were for me. In this way I wrench them away from God, towards whom they are actually directed, and for whom they actually exist. This is a deep degradation: a tree that is for God is a mythological being of great meaning, a bridge between realms, a place of connection between heaven and earth. A tree that is for me is only an externalization of some trivial fact about my emotional state at the time I encounter it. I cannot offer a tree the lofty destiny that God can, because I am not very lofty. But I don't stop there, because I often have in mind much more prosaic uses: it is material I can use to build my dreams. In this way, I turn a mighty tree into nothing more than lumber.

My encounters with people are also marked by calculation, converting individuals into their use-value to me. In such calculations, I set aside all that is particular and unique about a person, all that is most glorious and mysterious. Oh, I may pretend that I value this person because of the things that make them different from others, and that I desire by my love to help them be the best image of God they can be. But all too often, my desire to spend time with them is based on how they can make me feel or how they can further my self-image or fulfill my desires for the life I want to

---

[57] Michael Ende, *The Neverending Story* (Firebird: New York, 2005), 238.

lead. If I were selfless, I would not cling to them, and in so doing, drag them into my destructive spiral.

And this is another point: not only do I pursue people and things in ways that are destructive to them, but also in ways that are destructive to me. For when I pursue the lie that all things are for my purposes, I set myself up as an idol, an alternative and competitor god, an absolute good in myself. But to be an idol, a mere counterfeit god, is so much less than to be an image of the living God. I reduce myself from an instance of the crown and glory of material creation to an object of ridicule and scorn. Even more, I cut myself off from life, from truth, from the good, from the beautiful, from meaning and purpose: in short, from everything that makes all things worth anything.

In the day-to-day, none of this appetite for and spreading of destruction bothers me much. Because it seems natural and normal, I swim in these waters as unfeelingly as any fish. But there is a God in Israel, and I have opened myself to his influence; I even dare, in my ignorance, to pray that he would make me a better person. And so judgment comes, for what friend could stand by and watch as the one he loves buries himself in filth and disgrace? The judgment of God takes many forms, but they all have this in common: when we submit to them, they show us the true face of our sins.

These sins appear as a threefold horror and despair. First, I see clearly the nature of my actions towards my neighbors. Before judgment, I always flinched back from the full realization of what my actions were costing others. But now I am forced to face it head-on, to see that I have been a destroyer in their lives, that I have come through like a tornado, leaving ruins in my wake. I have done such evil to others that they may wonder if there can even be good in this world; I have broken their dreams and trampled on their hearts, and all the time I congratulated myself that my actions were love to them. But it is no love that destroys what it loves, and it is a cheap love that selfishly smothers and suffocates another's good because *my* delight in it is so great.

It would be easier for me if I did not truly love them at all. Then I bear only (!) the guilt of having harmed and degraded an image of God. But where I have truly loved, I have also wrought this destruction on one to whom I longed to bring good. Were anyone else to attempt such harm on these loved ones, I would rise up in righteous anger and interpose myself between them, even at the cost of my life. What can I do with the knowledge that *I* have done these things to them, that I have become an enemy of their souls, laid a snare for their feet, betrayed my love with the actions of hate? Everything they suffer because of me becomes a new wound in my soul, and one I do not want to escape before I have suffered sufficiently.

This point is only sharpened when I come to see clearly what I have been doing to myself: the fantasies and the trivialities with which I have delighted my soul turn out to be venom and filth of the most perverse sort. When I indulge in anger and unforgiveness, when I delight in lust and gluttony, when I wrap myself in deceit, when I revel in pride, or give in to unbelief: in all these things I am deforming and disfiguring my soul. My original and only beauty is to be this image of God, unrepeatable and irreplaceable, yet I turn my back on that, taking a hammer to the priceless statue for no reason that makes any good sense in the light of judgment. I have traded the glories of eternity for a pack of gum.

And that, I think, hurts the most: not the particular exchange, but the fact that I am the sort of person who would make such a fool's bargain. I cannot stand to see that I am a person who loves offal, who wraps shameful filth around himself as if it were silk, and proudly parades around. I have always thought myself noble, wise, *worthy* to be loved: now I know that I am the most ridiculous, pitiable, and vile thing in creation.

But it is this last step that breaks my heart beyond repair, for in it I come to see the truth of what David prayed: "Against you, you only, have I sinned" (Ps 51:4). This revelation does not invalidate the previous ones: I would rather translate this text as "against you *uniquely* have I sinned." I really have sinned against my neighbor and myself; I really harmed and damaged them, but that evil pales in comparison to what it offers to my God. Whatever harm I have done to others, I have done to God, and whatever hurt I have caused myself, I have caused him also: for who do I love more than him, and who loves me more? Who therefore could feel greater betrayal than he does, greater heartbreak over my loss and destruction, greater sympathy with my anguish? And a perfect and loving God feels these things not less, but more than a human can.

And then there is this, and (to be honest) when I truly see my guilt, I hate this: that he underwent the greatest agony possible to a human for me, that he *died* for me; that he forgave me before I asked, before I was even sorry, that even in the moment that I was breaking his heart most deeply, he was forgiving me.

But this can't be, for if he forgives me, he runs the risk of making light of all that I have done. There is also a risk that my victims will not get the justice they deserve, because I am not suffering as I ought. The gospel of Christ is good enough news to one who does not really understand sin and thus is able to accept forgiveness without too much trouble. But to the one who *does* understand sin and has been awakened to its severity and degradation, the gospel promise of remission is almost offensive: it seems to make light of sin, to excuse it, even. At a deep level, I do not *want* this forgiveness, because my sense of justice demands that the perpetrator be hanged, and because I can at least salvage some shred of personal honor in going willingly, in affirming that this is what I deserve, and by my dying (*my* dying, not his) in some small measure atone for what I have done.

That he should want to stop all that from happening is out of proportion with the nature of my sin, and borders on the offensive. And yet, only he can do this. I do not want him to die for my sin, I want to die for my own sin as the completion of my atonement. But this is just how I got into this mess in the first place: trying to replace God with myself, trying to take on myself what must be left to God alone. I cannot atone, not one iota. The ones who love me, however much I hurt them, are not served by my death: they are only further hurt in the face of what they can only interpret as an ultimate rejection, a final, senseless act of selfishness. For love does not atone by fleeing but by *abiding*.

But I cannot let go of my own sense of justice and shame: I am dead in my sins, and so I lack the agency I need to accept this gift of salvation. In such a situation, where I lie in the land of death and cannot accept the promise of life, how can even a resurrected God save me? This is what it feels like to be dead in my sin. But if the problem is death (even if my death in my sin), then we can confidently reply that even death won't stop him: Christ shows conclusively in his Passion that death is no barrier, that he is happy to cross that boundary to retrieve us if need be.

And yet what I want to point attention to is not so much that he died, but that he remained dead for three days. Christ did not just enter into death: he abode in it. In that abiding he plumbed death to its furthest depths, leaving no region untested, no area unexplored. In so doing, he brought death into his kingdom as a place where he is also revealed to be Lord: he now holds its keys.[58] Christ does not move among the dead as one defeated, aimless, or lost: he moves as one surveying a new realm, cataloging its every part, charting its future abolition. Christ in the land of the dead is *lordly*, or to use an equivalent word, *sovereign*.

---

[58] Rev 1:18

Let us return to the sinner dead in his sin (me). My problem is not that I am dead, but that I'm not dead *enough*. For Christ too is dead, and he is about to emerge victorious from that abiding in death. So to be dead is no bar to union with God, for it is no bar to *being* God. But unlike me, Christ is dead *to sin*. Those who are dead in their sins still cling to a half-life of self-sufficiency, evidenced by my desire to die my own atoning death. This is evidence that my sin still lives. I wish to die for it, but this accomplishes nothing, because I am its slave and it already owes me death as my wage.[59] No, the only path to freedom lies in dying *to* it, in letting go of my desire to make atonement or pay the price, in letting go of the last pretenses to self-sufficiency and choosing instead to follow the God-steps to the furthest regions of death. For it is only from there, at the outermost boundary of the land of the dead, that Christ will arise to new life. I have to meet him there if I would follow him back to the world of life.[60] My job is to let go, and *go*.

Thus it becomes clear that only a God who rose from the dead can save, because what was needed was for him to enter the realm of death and tread a path to resurrection that I could follow. Even this I do not do in my own strength: for where Christ is, all of God is, and so even my ability to follow his steps is empowered by the Holy Spirit he gives me. But now that I am on this path, I do not care what belongs to me and what belongs to God, for I have died to the desire to replace God with myself, to the desire to see any competition between God and myself. This desire is what held me in bondage and what made death seem so inescapable; but death is easily escaped: all you have to do is die.

We really see the world from the inside out.

---

[59] Romans 6:23

[60] Romans 6:11: "In the same way, count yourselves dead to sin but alive to God in Christ Jesus."

11

Meet Me at the Well

*"Love bade me welcome. Yet my soul drew back
Guilty of dust and sin.
But quick-eyed Love, observing me grow slack
From my first entrance in,
Drew nearer to me, sweetly questioning,
If I lacked any thing."*
George Herbert, "Love (III)"

*"As they pass through the Baca Valley,
he provides a spring for them.
The rain even covers it with pools of water.
They are sustained as they travel along;
each one appears before God in Zion."*
Ps 84:5–7 NET

Misery loves company. We've all heard that, haven't we?

But there is a little sentence tucked away in the New Testament that is the *version* to which "Misery loves company" is the *per*version: it's "Make my joy complete." The first thought says, "If I'm going to be miserable, so are you." The second says, "I found something wonderful, but I won't be really satisfied until you enter into the joy with me."

What compels the Christian? Guilt? Obligation? Rewards? For the Christian, joy is one of the central and defining characteristics of God's loving reality, a reality God has called "very good." And joy loves company. When the Samaritan woman sees Jesus seeing her, his love wells up within her, filling her with joy. Immediately, she hits the ground running, singing his praises. She wants someone else to know the joy too: to *make her joy complete*.

C.S. Lewis said that joy was different from happiness, and that it could even feel like a kind of grief, yet a kind of grief that you desire. A good ache. I don't think the ache could be called good if there weren't really some chance of making real, lasting contact with the source of that joy. And it certainly would have remained forever beyond our reach, if it had not first reached out to us. Love has shown its face, and it is the face of Jesus.

Singing is the word for most anything a soul does in grateful response to having been loved. It may be literal music-making, or it may be the weeping of glad tears in silence. Singing is a basket-word that holds all kinds of good fruit—many sorts of singing.

For a long time, joy was hard for me to believe in. A real death had occurred in my life, and that fruit was gone—or at least I'd lost the ability to taste it. It took many years for it to begin to grow again, and at times I'm amazed how tender the plant can be even now, when the weather is fussy. I'm amazed how much reassurance I need about what I've become so sure of.

When Jesus told the Samaritan woman that if she accepted the Living Water she'd never thirst again, I don't think he meant that her neediness would be erased, but that what she desired would always be there for her (and for us). He would personally see to it that we lack no good thing.

God knows the thirst doesn't go away, and that the joy sometimes does, in fact, feel more like thirst. More like an "inconsolable longing," as Lewis called it. The heartbreaks don't disappear, either. Instead, something new appears in their midst. Something like a well in the middle of the burning sands: a Face that meets you and me with a Word that washes over us like the music of Living Water, teaching our tired hearts to sing a song we'd thought impossible.

Meet Me at the Well

Every thirst we've cursed is leading to a Spring our maps misplaced
Like every human ache awoken in our broken hearts is grace
Tracing through the places we have dug in desperate thirst
To lead us to the Well who comes to meet us at our worst

Oh come, come and meet me at the Well
If you've tried your hand at love and failed
Come, come and meet me at the Well
Come drink the Living Water and be healed, come be healed

In the face of Christ there is a light revealing our disease
But the Lord of Peace has come to see the prisoners released
So pour upon this cracked earth Living Water, Lord, and shape
From willing clay a Living Bride revived before your Face

The day I saw you seeing me
That was the first time I could see
The truth that I was loved completely
I feel a new song coming on
I feel my lost heart coming home
Oh, let the whole world come and drink
And sing the song of the redeemed

Oh come, come and meet me at the Well
If you've tried your hand at love and failed
Come, come and meet me at the Well
Come drink the Living Water and be healed, come be healed

Come behold, come beloved, come be held, come be whole,
come be healed

The Digger's Tale
Rex Bradshaw

Like many boys, I loved to grab a shovel and dig. Beneath my half-acre backyard, I imagined, were hidden riches. The buried treasure I usually sought was dinosaur bones; nobody informed me until later that Oregon was ocean floor during the Mesozoic Era, but I do not think it would have mattered. I would have dug anyway.

I was routinely foiled by something called the water table. Water was the one thing I did not wish to find, but on the floor of the Willamette Valley, my hole rarely got deeper than a couple feet before it filled with brown groundwater, even in the driest part of summer.

Though I never found what I sought, whether a *Styracosaurus* skeleton or a portal to Bism, digging was a compulsion. I felt an urge to pierce the rind of the earth and discover what lay beneath it, to push the boundaries of my knowledge beyond the surface, to reach with both hands for subterranean mysteries.

Humans may be diggers by nature. The environment we shape is pocked by excavation, from the ancient wells of Cyprus to the chasmic gold mines of South Africa. In many cases, the treasure sought is well-defined, whether water, gold, or dinosaur bones. But for *Homo fodiens*, man as digger, the necessity of the search may be clearer than its object. As Plato pointed out long ago, we only seek what we lack: desire springs from a void we wish to fill. As existential diggers, that void might just be our *selves*.

We tend to see the self in terms of our private emotional lives, experienced through the chemical balance of our nervous systems. This "self" has certain innate hungers that we satisfy through eating, intimate touch, and the like. Our reward system eventually learns to respond to other activities as well: sports, shopping, video games, singing, receiving applause, and so forth.

But what happens when our understanding of our selves is restricted to this region of experience? Pleasures such as food, sex, and recognition gratify only up to a particular limit—yet this natural boundary leaves *Homo fodiens* unsatisfied, so we dig for more. Delving for dopamine becomes the occupation of our lives, as we explore familiar cavities of pleasure and dowse for new veins.

Early on, we pursue our subterranean quarry with eagerness; we squeeze the dirt for as much pleasure as will drip into our tin. The world, meanwhile, continually evokes in our mind new visions of delight, waiting just a few inches beneath the soil. Advertising, pornography, false religion, false activism—they whet our appetite with a steady stream of fantasies promising something new. Our economy is harnessed to these limitless consuming selves. The definition of satiety is forever expanding, and fear of missing out is fierce, forbidding us from settling down to enjoy our conquests. The carnival threatens to command our attention until the last heartbeat.

But sooner or later the contradictions dawn on us. Even as we wallow in self-indulgence, we are all the more prey to tedium, doubt, and insecurity. The void does not fill, and we realize that multiplication of finite goods gets us no closer to infinity. So we strive for prudence and moderation. We listen to the sages and experts who tell us to simplify our lives, to read good books, to build good habits, to nurture relationships, to put God first. Perhaps we even perceive that what we really long for is not phantom pleasure but *communion*, a sharing of life. We are not atoms, after all, but persons whose reality is relationship. *That* is the self that must be fulfilled, which cannot happen by exiling ourselves to islands of amusement or self-satisfaction.

We continue to dig, though now we dig for something else, something better. But something is wrong. Our lives are obstinately complicated, our books grant us only momentary escape, our habits do not last, our relationships are spoiled by selfishness, and God is silent. A hollowness yawns behind the self we act out. And what if others, behind their masks, are just as impoverished and grasping? In that case, their gestures toward us must be as empty and self-serving as our gestures toward them. And God? Perhaps God has been one of those phantasms of the lower self, a ghost of the imagination. God seems so small and inadequate now, a contrivance of our own selfish need. On inspection, we find little to suggest that a chaotic universe cares for us.

This moment, in which we raise our eyes from our excavations and blink under the sky, is a critical one. But the prospect is frightening. In the absence of *face*, the communication of a vital interior, the world is just *surface*, and the very idea of communion is meaningless. We approach the uncomfortable question: *What if there is no real treasure down there?*

Most of us would prefer to shut down this line of thought before we strike the rock of nihilism. But hope lingers. Sometimes, as we dig about with clearer vision but dimmer purpose, we turn up moments that pierce our weary hearts. We fall in love. We see oak leaves rippling in late-afternoon sunlight. We hear the laughter of our children. Something, or someone, appears to be reaching out toward us; the boundary-line between our heart and the world grows hazy. But when the touch of beauty passes, it leaves a wound that exposes the disorder and ugliness within. We are still hard and proud and addicted to our own desires.

We look back over our lives, all the half-finished holes filled with stagnant water, and if we do not deceive ourselves, it is a depressing sight. We spy the familiar old well of religion. Perhaps we have tasted its water before. Some of us may recall the bitter sulfuric odor of the family tap, the taint of intolerance or abuse. In any case, it did not sate us, and we grew thirsty again. There is no treasure to be found here—just water and darkness.

But the traveler stops nearby. We assume he is a digger, like us; his cloak is stained by the mud of a road he may have followed for millennia.

"Give me a drink."

We stare down at the dirty, useless water our shovels have exposed. Why would he ask *us* for water? Does he really want this? Is he trying to shame us?

"If you knew the gift of God, and who it is who says to you, 'Give me a drink,' you would have asked him, and he would have given you living water. Whoever drinks of the water that I will give him shall never thirst; but the water that I will give him will become in him a well of water springing up to eternal life."[61]

Now we look at him with suspicion. Does this traveler know something we do not? Where is this "living water" supposed to come from? Is he just another well-water salesman, trying to pass his swill off as treasure?

To our surprise, he looks us in the eyes. He sees us, and we see him seeing us, holding us in love. In that shared gaze, a space opens for the communion we had thought impossible, inviting us forward.

What holds us back? Do we still imagine our own shovels will eventually turn up something of value? Or do we yet doubt the promise of those eyes? Does the wound of desire pain us so much

---

[61] John 4:7, 10, 13-14

that we recoil toward disappointment and shame? Are we afraid to lose our false selves on the threshold of his fullness of being?

Nevertheless, as we hold the stranger's loving gaze, our skins of despair start to fall away. This just might be a treasure hid in the field, a hope worth embracing. As we start to let ourselves believe, reality gains dimension and transparency. If he is true, the universe is no Potemkin village; beneath it wells a profound love, his very heart's blood pouring across the divide our desire could not bridge. We see in him the living water that courses through the arteries of creation, the love that moves the sun and other stars.

There is nothing for it, but to take his living water and drink.

I have described here, in the form of a parable, one path to a transformative encounter with Jesus; there are other routes, I believe, more or less circuitous. My journey since earliest childhood has taken place within the church, but it only began in earnest when I learned to mark and follow the line of beauty, hoping it ran toward the truth. A decade on, I am a beginner and a digger still, but the way leads me in a golden spiral, always back to the fountain of his grace.

The ultimate place of *Homo fodiens* is before the crucified and exalted Christ. In his broken body, a portal has opened into the living depths of reality that none of our shovels could reach. We have been shown the love of heaven, love that rises to meet us at each footstep.

This love has not yet come to maturity in us. It must be tested if it is to blossom into infinity; that is the Spirit's concern. But first we must dare to take the nuptial chalice, to surrender the self of isolation and put on Christ, to share in his life. Within our opened hearts, the holy spring rises up. We need no longer dig wells, but vineyards of work and prayer. Our Lord, the stranger at the well, stands ready with his own instruments to take in hand the cratered terrain of our lives and make of it a garden.

EPILOGUE:
Gentleness Towards Each Face

Matthew Clark

A Word from a Mute Boy

Many years ago, a friend and I drove to Atlanta to see a Cirque du Soleil show. We got there early and found our seats. There was a young man in the row in front of me, and for a brief moment he turned around and our eyes met. This will be impossible for me to describe, but something astonishing came through this boy's face and was indelibly imprinted on my spirit. I saw a holy presence. It was immediately clear to me that he was a special needs boy, though we never spoke; in fact, I don't think he was able to speak. His face was the only word he gave, and that was far more than I could take in.

I never learned anything more about him other than what I could glimpse in those few moments of eye contact. But it was a transfiguring instance. His face showed no smudge, no darkness.

Through his countenance came a light bearing an intensity of innocence that shook me deeply with its beauty. It was at once disarming, discomfiting, utterly peaceful and present, and incandescent with love. All the music, dance, and joy of the Cirque du Soleil show that followed, breathtaking as it was, seemed like a mere adornment to that moment of being faced by that mute boy.

What is a Face?

One autumn while I was on tour, I passed through the Wisconsin Dells and camped for a night or two. I sat beside my little fire as the Milky Way bloomed above me and stars adorned the dark pine crowns like glimmering jewels. The constant thrum of cricket music and frog voices melded with the crackle of burning branches amidst the embers. The Mississippi River, early in its long journey down past my home state to the gulf, whispered in the night not far away. All creation around me seemed to deal out a gracious invitation to recognize the living presence of its Creator, and I sang quietly before sleep, "Praise Him, all creatures here below."[62]

In his poem "As Kingfishers Catch Fire," G. M. Hopkins describes how each mortal thing "deals out that being indoors each one dwells—selves," and he lands this whole idea on the last word of the poem: *faces*. The instant a kingfisher emerges from the water to catch the fire of the sunlight, flickering for one bright moment, we briefly glimpse a face from beyond nature crossing the threshold of creation. Hopkins's term for this is *selving*: "Each mortal thing . . . selves," he says. ". . . *myself* it speaks and spells." In so doing, it also speaks and spells the name of its source of being: Christ ("for Christ plays in ten thousand places").

---

[62] Thomas Ken, "Praise God from Whom All Blessings Flow." Public Domain.

If Hopkins is right about *selving*, then everything God has made, by "acting in God's eye what in God's eye [it] is" manifests in this world something of God's immaterial "face." If crickets, stars, and rivers can do that, how much more the human? So God has invented in the human face a wondrous resting place—a habitation—for his glory. In its features, Hopkins says, we see Christ at play to the Father's glory and for his revealing. Ultimately, this truth is fully realized in Jesus, where we discover "the light of the knowledge of the glory of God in the face of Jesus Christ" (2 Cor 4:6 ESV).

Face, then, is an uncreated relational reality from "before all worlds"; the members of the Trinity face one another. In the fullness of time, the Incarnation of Jesus became the consummation and the deepest fulfillment of God's intention for the human face. To turn and face the God who is facing us in Jesus Christ is to be ratified; to see him seeing us is to learn to see ourselves truly, as well as to be given our true self in him, in the light of his face.

Like Seeing the Face of God

In his book, *Self and Salvation: Being Transformed*,[63] David Ford explores salvation in terms of the face, saying:

> Christianity is characterised by the simplicity and complexity of facing: being faced by God, embodied in the face of Christ; turning to face Jesus Christ in faith; being members of a community of the face; seeing the face of God reflected in creation and especially in each human face, with all the faces in our heart related to the presence of the face of Christ; having an ethic of *gentleness towards each face* . . . [64] (italics mine)

---

[63] I'm especially grateful to the painter Bruce Herman for recommending Ford's book, which laid some of the groundwork for *Ordinary Saints*, a collaborative project between Bruce Herman, poet Malcolm Guite, and composer J. A. C. Redford. Find out more at the website: https://ordinary-saints.com.
[64] Ford, 24–25.

In a world so marred by sin, I search the dark mirror for my own face, but find it can only distort and smudge my features. The entropies of loneliness and fear are the best I can muster for myself, and only the face of Jesus can reflect back to me the healing reality of my belovedness. Like the woman who laid a hand to the hem of Jesus' garment and was healed, we'll never discover the beautiful truth until we find ourselves held in the loving gaze of God in Christ.

The Apostle John, who laid his head on Jesus' chest, assures us that "the Son of God has come and given us understanding so that we can know the one who is true. And we are in the one who is true, since we are in his Son Jesus Christ. [Jesus] is the true God and eternal life" (1 John 5:20). We truly can know the Father, since Jesus has made him known. The Invisible God and the Incarnate Jesus who faces us correspond perfectly: the loving face Jesus shows us truly is God's.

We meet our true selves in his face. When treacherous Jacob finally goes to face his brother Esau, he fully expects to be destroyed, yet he is surprised to find himself forgiven and embraced. Jacob says that seeing the forgiveness in his brother's face is "like seeing the face of God" (Gen 33:10). Jacob has been living with that fear for twenty years. Can you imagine the relief? Likewise, we discover the shocking good news of God's enduring love for us only when, in spite of the legion of condemning voices, we finally dare turn our faces to meet his "sweet and gracious eye."[65]

Like Jacob, the Samaritan woman at the well in John 4 experiences such an instance of discovery by the end of her conversation with Jesus. What she sees in the face of our Lord changes everything. She meets her true self in his face; every sad name falls away as Jesus claims her as his Beloved. Her heart feathers out into glorious song, and she becomes the "first evangelist." The lover—and only the lover—sings.

---

[65] George Herbert and Ann Pasternak Slater, "The Glance," *The Complete English Works*. (New York: Knopf, 1995), 167.

The Cost of Looking the Other Way

You've never met a liar
You've only met the lie that they put forth
There ain't no soul more lonely
Until you tell the truth you can't be touched

One of life's deepest griefs is that not every encounter with Jesus ends with the lover singing. If we don't allow ourselves to be seen, we cannot be enfolded into reality. But it's a vulnerable thing, since being seen—even as it welcomes us—asks something of us. "[The *face*] is primarily an ethical relation in which I find myself summoned to responsibility for the one who appeals to me."[66]

In other words, a face interrogates us, which makes integration with others possible.[67] If we aren't willing to welcome the face that calls us to responsibility, we exclude ourselves from participation in reality; we turn our backs on the healing real love makes available, losing ourselves and our minds.[68] Jesus assures us that reality—the King and his kingdom—are readily available to those who will repent and lay hold of him, for the kingdom is *at hand* (within reach).

Pilate can't make sense of Jesus' otherworldly responses to his questions. Over the course of their encounter, Pilate grows uneasy, gradually realizing that he is the one being interrogated. He dismisses Jesus, saying, "What is truth?" (John 18:38). From that point on, I imagine Pilate avoiding eye contact with the Lord as he turns his face from Jesus, washing his hands of the whole affair. But Pilate cannot understand, overcome, or extinguish the light of that face. He can only hide his own face and pass untouched and untouchable into the void.

---

[66] Ford, 37.
[67] Ford, 3.
[68] Paranoia means to be *para* (beside/out of) your *noia* (mind). To reject reality leads to paranoia; to turn toward reality is to *meta* (turn/change) your *noia* (mind); *metanoia* is the New Testament word for repentance.
[69] C. S. Lewis, *The Four Loves* (Orlando: Harcourt, Brace., 1991), 121.

The only place outside of heaven where we may be entirely safe from the interrogating face of love is hell.[69] "What is truth?"—such a safe and despairing thing to say. Pilate asks the question as someone who has stopped looking for the answer. Unlike the Samaritan woman at the well, he won't abide the Holy Questioner, choosing instead to remain entombed forever in the dark safety of lies, never to be touched by the warming presence of the "true light that gives light to everyone" (John 1:9).

Sarah Clarkson points out that when God questions Job, it is not meant to crush him, but to open his eyes to a vast vision of beauty that would quench his thirst in the midst of despair:

> [Job confesses] that "I had heard of you by the hearing of the ear, but now my eye has seen you" (42:5), an awed and grateful wondering that makes him capable of recognizing God's presence and power at work in the broken world . . . The history of suffering shifts as Job steps into the light of God's presence, as he lifts his face to look upon the God who has arrived in the midst of his suffering with a beauty that cannot be gainsaid and a light that cannot be quenched.[70]

God faces us to free us—to break the snare of the fowler.

Faces at the Table

Alexander Schmemann says we are hungry beings[71] and our life comes from receiving the given life of another. In my essay on the cross, I told the story of killing a deer when I was a kid. That was a vivid experience of the reality Schmemann is pointing out. I saw that, in the death my hands had wrought of a beautiful creature, its life would be given over to sustain mine. Kneeling beside a dying doe in that dusky field that day, an echo of the Eucharist stirred upon the wind with the words, "Take and eat; this is my body" (Matt 26:26).

---

[70] Sarah Clarkson, *This Beautiful Truth: How God's Goodness Breaks into Our Darkness* (Baker Books, 2021), 206.
[71] Alexander Schmemann, *For the Life of the World* (New York: St. Vladimir's Seminary Press, 1982), 14.

Schmemann goes on to say that "the world was created as . . . the material of one all-embracing Eucharist, and man was created as the priest of this cosmic sacrament."[72] God has given the world to us as a kind of food to be offered back in gratitude, as a means of communion, to God. Jesus is, of course, the Great High Priest, who fulfills humanity's priestly calling. Answering his invitation to join him at his Table reincorporates us into that calling, which is at the heart of what God always purposed for us. The Lord's Table re-weds us to life's true form, demonstrated at the cross: that there is no greater love than to lay down one's life for another.

When we sidle up to that Table, we behold the face of Jesus, who shows us the way the Father looks at us. We also see those seated around the table with us, our companions (*companion* is a word that means "those who share the same bread"). We wind up held and beheld in a great symphony of beholding. We break bread and keep the feast, only to find the whole world at our fingertips as a means of enacting and extending, as a great thanksgiving in Christ, God's way of living.

In this life, we pass so many starved faces for whom the Lord has offered the bread of his body. We were created to love as we have been loved, which means that we look to others in order to see ourselves, and the Lord's love, often through us, can hold a chalice to someone's parched lips.

A Pilgrimage of Beholding

Once when I was playing some house concerts in the Midwest, several people recommended that I visit the Cincinnati Zoo during the few days I'd have off that next week. It was a blast! I wandered around by myself all day long, and one of my favorite parts was feeding the giraffes. I'd never been so close up to a giraffe's face before and had no idea how enormous their heads are. I find them wonderful and hilarious. When I look at a giraffe,

---

[72] Schmemann, 15.

I can see traces of God's personality; "Someone has been here," I say to myself laughing, though the animal itself is not a person. But with a human, I say, "Someone has been here, and someone is, in fact, here!" The Creator God has left his coinage, and something more than mere flesh stands before me. This is a living person, an image-bearer with eternity set in her heart.[73]

In his book *The Face of God*, the late Roger Scruton says that when we look at a human face, we discover that some personal presence from beyond the material world has crossed a threshold into materiality.[74] In other words, we search a face to discover whether we are looking at a *thing* or a *person*. Here, "the distinction between spirit and matter disappears, as it does in the Sacraments. For here I experience the oddity that flesh is the mode under which I apprehend the truth of the thing. It is the epiphany of the thing . . . the human body is the epiphany of personhood."[75] That epiphany is most concentrated in the face.

Josef Pieper says that much is at stake unless we can learn again to see, *to behold*, for "the ultimate fulfillment, the absolutely meaningful activity, the most perfect expression of being alive, the deepest satisfaction, and the fullest achievement of human existence must needs happen in an instance of beholding."[76] That's a mouthful, but Pieper's effusive litany is fitting; he's pointing out that beholding as contemplation is key to recovering our lost humanity. Take a close look at the word *contemplate*; do you notice the word *temple* tucked in there? That's no accident. A temple is a threshold place within creation, set aside to house the presence of a god, and it is where you go to focus your attention upon the deity's presence—to give your eyes to seeing and your ears to hearing.

---

[73] Eccl 3:11

[74] "My face is a boundary, a threshold, the place where I appear as a monarch appears on the balcony of a palace." Roger Scruton, *The Face of God* (London: Bloomsbury Continuum, 2014), 78.

[75] Thomas Howard, *Chance or the Dance: A Critique of Modern Secularism* (San Francisco: Ignatius Press, 2001), 120, 126. Howard is referring specifically to sexual consummation here, which is a particularly intimate instance of facing. His point is that more than just a physical act is taking place; two spiritual persons manifest and interface as bodies.

[76] Josef Pieper, *Only the Lover Sings: Art and Contemplation* (San Francisco: Ignatius Press, 1990), 22.

The writer of Psalm 27 says that he wishes for one thing above all else: "to dwell in the Lord's house all the days of my life, so I can gaze at the splendor of the Lord and contemplate in his temple." Then he concentrates his desire even further, putting it in terms of the face: "My heart says 'Seek his face!' Oh, Lord, your face I do seek!" To contemplate is to wait upon the Lord in his holy temple and to "gaze upon his beauty" (Ps 27:4, 8 NET).

Like the bud turned towards the sun blooms, the woman at the well beholds Jesus' face and becomes the lover who sings. She discovers that at the heart of reality is a grand sing-along, a great resounding call to respond with our voices to the God whose beauty has given voice to our being. The invitation to join in this song appears in Jesus' face, which tunes us to reality.[77] And we must be re-tuned to reality because we were created to play within a cosmic symphony of God's composing, but we are instruments long fallen out of tune and warped by misuse. We've grown tone-deaf, tuneless, and without a tuning fork and the skill of a master luthier, how can we ever hope to sing in tune again, taking our place in the most beautiful of songs? To face Jesus opens a way for the instrument to be healed. The song can be recovered. We can be restored to his likeness and our place in the orchestra of holy harmony. "When he appears we shall be like him"[78] means that, like Pieper says, the "fullest achievement of human existence" is realized when we finally meet Jesus face to face.

Seeing the face of God, in traditional terms, is called the Beatific Vision[79]—it is the consummation of humanity's existence, our destiny, our *telos*. How can I be emphatic enough? All that is has been invited on pilgrimage[80] towards this singularly glorious

---

[77] Once tuned, an instrument is freed to play. Play opens up the responsive possibilities of improvisation within the integrity of a given song, followed by collaboration, expression, resonance, harmony, and on and on.
[78] 1 John 3:2
[79] Hans Boersma, *Seeing God: The Beatific Vision in Christian Tradition* (Grand Rapids: Eerdmans, 2018).
[80] "For man, to 'be' means to 'be on the way'—he cannot be in any other form; man is intrinsically a pilgrim." Pieper goes on to describe the destination of humankind's pilgrimage as union with the greatest good, God. Pieper, 42.

point of contact with God himself; this union is the indescribable joy set before those of us who, trusting in Christ, have set our hearts on pilgrimage.[81]

The Courage to Look

I can hardly recall a time when the stories of J. R. R. Tolkien were not a part of my life. From my earliest days, elves, hobbits, wizards, and dragons were laid alongside the Lord's Prayer and a kiss from my mother at bedtime. All these years later, few things give me a deeper sense of being at home in this world than visiting that other world of Middle Earth.

In *The Lord of the Rings*, the main villain contrasts sharply with the Christian invitation to the joy of contemplative beholding. Sauron's single eye represents a mono-vision bent solely on power and possessiveness. Beholding, on the other hand, calls us to open both eyes and meet face to face in a context of freeing-belonging[82] and vulnerability—not to dominate another, but to love them and seek their good. "To contemplate . . . means to open one's eyes receptively to whatever offers itself to one's vision, and the things seen enter into us, so to speak, without calling on any effort or strain on our part to possess them."[83] That kind of looking may be one of the most terrifying things in the world because it makes us so vulnerable.

We mediate that kind of contact with faces in many ways, but most recently through the safety of our screens. George Steiner says "we seek the immunities of indirection"; we ache for contact, but the direct encounter with a *real presence* is too scary. We look for ways to buffer interactions—to achieve the safety of immunity

---

[81] Ps 84:5
[82] Real freedom is always situated within and enabled by what Wendell Berry and Eugene Peterson call "membership." St. Paul gave the analogy of the Body of Christ in both 1 Cor. 12:12-26 and Rom 12:3-8, since, being made for loving communion, freedom is only available to us within the context of mutual belonging and responsibility.
[83] Josef Pieper and Alexander Dru, *Leisure: The Basis of Culture; The Philosophical Act* (San Francisco: Ignatius Press, 2009), 26.

by making all of our contact indirect. Social media works all too well in this regard. We're just beginning to discover how lonely and anxious it is making us.

The face of another person is, by good design, beautifully intrusive. The face is always calling into question our "immunities of indirection,"[84] by virtue of the "real presence" it transmits. When that mute boy before the Cirque du Soleil show looked at me, I felt a kind of collapse in my defenses; a curtain tore and a holy presence poured across the threshold of his face into my spirit. His gaze was one of absolute vulnerability and absolute trust.

We also buffer ourselves by what Steiner calls "today's idolatry of the 'informational.'"[85] In a climate of fear we look for ways to manufacture safety (this comprises a great deal of the culture of marketing). But how do you remove the risk from relationship? You must shrink a person to something less than an immortal being gifted with incomprehensible transcendence.[86] Reducing persons to comprehensible collections of data has its advantages, but real contact is "irreducible to reason or pragmatic reckoning."[87] To whittle the vastness of personhood down to ones and zeros is an attempt to make the wild, unfathomable depths of the Spirit (who blows where he wills—quite beyond our control) seem a little more manageable. This kind of inhospitable reduction of people is the opposite of *facing*; it's *de-facing*.

The cost of control and invulnerability is high. Like Sauron's, our vision narrows, and love withers; *defaced* people become objects and obstacles to manage (and ultimately dominate). On the other hand, vulnerability opens us to friendship as our own lives become more fruitful and felicitous than they could have been alone, and people become companions. Tolkien's protagonists find courage in

---

[84] George Steiner, *Real Presences* (University of Chicago Press, 1989), 39.
[85] Steiner, 43.
[86] C. S. Lewis, *The Weight of Glory and Other Addresses* (New York: HarperCollins, 2001), 45–46.
[87] Steiner, 19.

fellowship and beauty, refusing to use power to avoid vulnerability. Rather than dominate or possess, they fight to trust one another. As companions *facing* each other in suffering, they are enabled to face evil together.

Where will we find the courage to be vulnerable?

It is a choice between idolatry or worship *in spirit and truth.* As we attempt to sidestep vulnerability, idolatry offers us the illusion of safety by reducing God to a persona we can possess and dominate. Idolatry is a set of practices, magic words, rain-dances, and procedures concocted to manipulate an unreliable deity. The idea is that if you do the rain-dance just right, the god will be obligated to comply. If you say the right words of faith, you can exercise power over reality. And the tragedy of idolatry would be our only option, if God hadn't proven himself to be so willing to join us in our vulnerability and commit himself so fully to our well-being.

At Sinai, Yahweh assures his people of two things: 1) that he can't be manipulated, and 2) that because he is trustworthy and good, manipulation is unnecessary. Idolatry is exhausting; his lovingkindness means they can finally rest. Rather than fearfully hiding behind screens in an anesthetized and buffered existence, God's trustworthiness and proven love set us free to deeply face all things with wonderful courage.

That proven love shows up at the cross, where the Lord, in his own vulnerability, companions us in suffering with the broken, shared bread of his own body.

Gentleness towards Each Face

My friend Jessie, who walked the Camino trail in Spain, told me that her favorite Spanish word is *mirada,* which means "the look in one's eyes." Now, I love to play with word connections, and often a single word can germinate into a rich range of connotations.

I wondered whether Jessie's favorite word might branch out in some fruitful ways with regard to the idea of facing. And lo and behold, it did!

It turns out that *mirar* sprouts out into: *mirror, miracle, wonder*, even *to look* and *to contemplate, to regard, to smile* or *laugh*.[88] I got excited watching this one word harmonizing so many ideas across this essay (and this album). Now, hold *mirar* one hand, and open your palm to hold another word: *gentleness*.

I remember standing in front of Bruce Herman's painting of his late dad for a long time. I was captivated by that father's face so tenderly represented by his own son. "Nobody has to observe and study the visible mystery of a human face more than the one who sets out to [paint] it."[89] It wasn't until later that I ran across the little phrase that I quoted earlier from the David Ford book that Bruce recommended: "gentleness towards each face."

Gentleness is a word that has to do with inheriting the likeness of those from whom you were generated: your parents. *Gene-* is the root of *genesis, generate, generation, genteel, gentle*. These are words about origins, birth and family patterns. Gentleness is handed down by birth and fostered by family. Maybe it's a basket-word that cradles all kinds of good family fruit. We are made in God's image and called his sons and daughters; gentleness means to bear the family likeness by carrying on the pattern of loving as we have been loved.

The songs and essays here catalog a two-way search. We look for the face that came looking for us beside a well in Samaria. At the close of this little book, we hold in one hand *mirar*; in the other, *gentleness*. We wonder at the miracle of being called God's Beloved Bride, destined to be united to him forever.

When we turn to face Jesus, then we have beheld *mirar*: "the look in God's eyes" towards us. Seeing his face mirrors back to

---

[88] According to my favorite word-nerd site: https://www.etymonline.com/search?q=mirar
[89] Pieper, *Only the Lover*, 35.

us the truth about where we came from and where we are going. Something we thought impossible suddenly becomes wondrously, miraculously possible: out of our apparent barrenness, new birth into God's Family.

When we turn to face Jesus in faith we are met with *gentleness*: we are re-generated (born again) into a new family. The Word who became flesh and dwelt among us makes available for us a new generative reality. Each of us is faced with the miracle of a second genesis, where we are forgiven in the light of his face and called "very good" again. Our Father offers this gladdening light to us in the face of his Son, and the Holy Spirit, like a Candle lighting a candle, offers that face through us as we bravely face the world with God's beautiful countenance.

The LORD bless you and keep you;
the LORD make his face shine on you
and be gracious to you;
the LORD turn his face toward you
and give you peace.

Num 6:24-26

Acknowledgments

Nothing good comes about without the love and help of many friends, and once you start attempting to trace the threads of gratitude, that fabric very quickly grows vast. Few things are more beautiful to me than seeing how God "sets the lonely in families" (Ps 68:6), as I have seen in my own life time after time. There are so many through whom the light of God's face has been revealed, making good work possible.

Steve and Terri Moon gave me a place in their hearts, in their home, and around their table, sharing not only the gospel of God but their very lives as well.[90] Without their hospitality, this project would not have happened. Lancia and Peter Smith have welcomed me into their home on many occasions over the years, and without Lancia's love as a companion in grief and her determined insistence on encouraging and challenging me as a writer, I would have lost heart with regard to God's calling. Some of these songs were written in Clay and Sally Clarkson's home; their affirmation and friendship have been invaluable these last many years. I always leave their presence feeling that more good is possible than I had thought.

I owe much to The Anselm Society and The Cultivating Project as communities of faithful imagination. Brian and Christina Brown of Anselm have sustained a conversation of creative renewal in the

---

[90] 1 Thess 2:8

church that has put food in my body and earth beneath my feet. Lancia Smith and my fellow Cultivators have written courageously with little reward, so that in a world "seared with trade; bleared, smeared with toil" tender things might find root and grow as witnesses to the Everlasting Kingdom.

Diana Glyer was among the first to whom I tossed out the idea of this book, and she gave such clear encouragement and practical advice that I began to believe it might not be such a dumb idea as I had thought! Dr. Glyer's scholarship and writing on the Inklings has also been invaluable; she supplied many of the tools (hope among them) that I needed to enter more willingly into collaboration.

Speaking of collaboration, The Draftlings is our Inklings-inspired writing group, and what a gift to have trusted friends with whom to share works-in-progress, knowing I can count on generosity, honesty, and invigorating challenge. Thank you, Rex Bradshaw, Sara Bannerman, Sam Clark, Jacob Rowan, Lindsay Gill, and John Barnts. For prayers, friendship, and a *home-in-the-world,* many thanks to The Fellowship, our weekly small group: Annie and Grace Andrews, Care McFaul, Tori Natale, along with Sam, Sara, and Rachael and Danielle Boxill.

Over coffee, Anita Palmer was God's provision of a renewed sense of purpose and possibility for this project. She didn't know it, but I was drooping, and her confidence and faith gave me faith to keep going.

The work of Malcolm Guite has, for more than a decade, been like the upending of Seamus Heaney's rain stick ("The Rain Stick" is one of the first poems I ever heard him talk about). I'm deeply grateful to Malcolm for how he has helped me, in deadly dried-out places, to listen again for "a music I never would have known to listen for" and to "begin the song exactly where" I was.

My brother Sam deserves big thanks because his warm-heartedness and welcome in the years since my life blew apart have been critical, his gift of hilarity has helped lift many a soil-stuck stone of sadness, his sincere openness to the Lord has refreshed me, and his humility has given me courage to keep coming home.

Bubba and Eva Humphrey may be total jerks for moving all the way to Texas just because the Lord called them to serve a church there, but, even so, they're some of my dearest friends. From the start, they made me a part of their family in a deep and beautiful way, and have been a resource for my imagination of God's redemptive reality and a refuge for my heart.

Years ago, after a season of total exhaustion, Emily Smith and Jill McClusky both confronted me about my tendency to work too much alone, and challenged me to invite friends to partner with me in ministry. Eventually, that became my Patron Partner team, whose prayers and gifts have been so life-giving, making this project and the day-to-day practicalities of life as an artist possible for several years now. John McCullough was among the very first to approach me with a desire to help, and I am especially grateful for his initiative, faith, and support. Jill has continued to be a regular sounding-board and dear friend. I also have in mind others from my church family: Steve Williams, Jimmy Young, B. G. Allen, Natalie and Erik Pinter, Barbara and Amy Ashcraft, Linda Williams, and Eileen Moorman.

Longtime friends Abbye and Jeff Pates kept the light of God's face before me in some of the darkest times of my life, though their hospitality cost them much. Katie Heckel, Oliver and Kate Box, Jay and Janna Knight, Jon David Cole, Matt King, Diana and Bill Bridgeman, Brian Mulder, and Adrienne Rogers have been precious friends to me. The healing process that resulted in these songs has a lot to do with their love over many years.

Rachel and Stephen Mosley have given me another *home-in-the-world*, making me a part of their family in ways that ease and give joy to my heart (including, but not limited to, living room dance parties).

Many thanks to my wonderful "Listening Team," the little group of folks who responded when I asked for feedback on the songs way back in the drafting and development stage, especially Sarah Tisdale, Care McFaul, Matthew Cyr, Megan Prahl, Kirstin Jeffrey Johnson, Athena Williams, May Novalis, Linda Rogers, and Stephen Mosley.

I am grateful to the Lord for Luke and Emily Ash, Kevan Chandler, Richard Grant, Brian Rushing, my parents (Susan and Joe Clark), Ashok and Neha Philip, Tom Frazier, Andrew and Cara Best, Vicki Stephens, Carson Murphy, Christa Wells, Mike and Allie Murphy, and all the wonderful musicians who brought these songs to life.

There are many authors and artists whose works have informed this project, among them: David Ford, Josef Peiper, Roger Scruton, Jonathan Rogers, Bruce Herman, and J. A. C. Redford.

To the essayists who have given so generously and worked so hard, taking a chance on this little project with me, how can I thank you enough for lending your voices to the telling of this story? Thank you, Andrew, Lanier, Amy, Adam W., Rex, Adam N., Heidi, Théa, Jessie, and Junius. Many thanks to our wonderful editor, Elisabeth Adams, who gracefully wrangled a pile of essays into a book.

This is the point where I realize it's not possible to thank everyone who deserves it! The cup overflows and the beauty of the outpouring of abundance God makes of our thirst becomes impossible to adequately communicate.

But I ought not forget to thank *you*. Thanks for picking up this book, for listening to this album. I hope you find in them a little of the abundance I've experienced in making them.

Contributors

Andrew Roycroft

Andrew Roycroft is a pastor and a poet from Northern Ireland. He is married to Carolyn and the father of two wonderful daughters. Andrew's big interests lie in theology and literature, and their capacity to point us towards God, his gospel, and his glory. Andrew serves as pastor of Portadown Baptist Church in County Armagh, and as a visiting lecturer in Biblical Theology and Apologetics at the Irish Baptist College. He also is privileged to provide regular contributions to The Rabbit Room website. His poetry has appeared in a variety of literary journals, and has been featured in community arts projects in Northern Ireland, in collaborative work with New Irish Arts, and in radio broadcasts with the BBC.

Lanier Ivester

Lanier Ivester is a homemaker and writer in the beautiful state of Georgia, where she maintains a small farm with her husband, Philip, and an ever-expanding menagerie of cats, dogs, sheep, goats, chickens, ducks, and peacocks. She studied English Literature at the University of Oxford, and her special areas of interest include the intersection of Christianity and art, the sacramental nature of everyday life, and the truth-bearing witness of the imagination. For over a decade she has kept a web journal at lanierivester.com, and her work has also been featured on The Rabbit Room, Art House America, The Gospel Coalition, and The Cultivating Project, among others. She has lectured across the country on topics ranging from the meaning of home to the integration of faith and reason, and in both her writing and her speaking she seeks to honor the holy longings of a homesick world.

Théa Rosenburg

Théa Rosenburg has worked as a dental assistant, an indie musician, a peddler of handknit gifts, an art teacher, an informal librarian, and an editor. She is a regular contributor to Story Warren; her work has also appeared on The Rabbit Room, Risen Motherhood, Deeply Rooted, and in *Wildflowers Magazine*. Théa lives with her husband and four daughters in the Pacific Northwest where, when the wind blows from the right direction, she can smell the ocean from her front yard. She reviews children's books for her blog, Little Book, Big Story.

Adam Whipple

Adam Whipple is a songwriter, multi-instrumentalist, composer, poet, and author releasing records and writings into the world from his home in East Tennessee. The founding editor of the arts journal Foundling House (2015-2021), his work has also appeared in The Rabbit Room, Curator Magazine, Blue Mountain Review, and the hometown Knoxville lit mag *The Pigeon Parade Quarterly*.

He has one patient wife, four bright children, five clueless chickens, and a tendency to wax eloquent about compost.

Heidi White

Heidi White, M. A., is a teacher, editor, podcaster, and author. She teaches Humanities at St. Hild School in Colorado Springs. She is the Managing Editor of FORMA Journal and a contributing author, blogger, and speaker at the CiRCE Institute. She is contributing author to *30 Poems to Memorize (Before It's Too Late)*, published by the CiRCE Institute. She is a weekly contributor on fiction, poetry, and Shakespeare on the Close Reads Podcast Network. She serves on the Board of Directors of The Anselm Society as well as sitting on the Academic Advisory Board for the Classical Learning Test. She writes fiction, poetry, and essays, and she speaks about literature, education, and the Christian imagination. She lives in Black Forest, Colorado, with her husband and children.

Matthew Clark

Matthew Clark is a singer/songwriter and storyteller from Mississippi. He has recorded several full-length albums, including a Bible walk-through called "Bright Came the Word from His Mouth" and "Beautiful Secret Life," a collection of songs highlighting, in George Herbert's phrase, "heaven in ordinary." Matthew hosts a weekly podcast, "One Thousand Words—Stories on the Way," featuring essays reflecting on faith-keeping. A musician and speaker, Matthew travels sharing songs and stories. Whether it's a song, a podcast, a meal, or an essay, Matthew loves to "make things that make room for people to meet Jesus."

Jessie Todd

Jessie Todd lives in Cleveland, Ohio, and works as a labor and delivery nurse by night and an amateur essayist by day. She has an English degree from Grove City College, and worked as a middle school English teacher at Evangelical Christian Academy in Madrid, Spain for several years before getting her nursing degree. She authors a newsletter called The Melancholy Monthly, and you can find those newsletters and her other work at themelancholymonthly.wordpress.com. She enjoys spending her free time walking and running through the Cuyahoga National Park, cooking any and all things autumnal, and caring for her many house plants.

Adam R. Nettesheim

Adam wanders through the arts as a vagabond. Though he still hasn't found what he's looking for, his travels have shown him that God has been weaving the golden thread of his story through our stories since the beginning, and he's not done yet. Adam and his wife Sarah have three children and live in Northern Colorado.

Amy Baik Lee

Amy Baik Lee writes from a desk looking out on a cottage garden, usually surrounded by children's drawings, teacups, and stacks of patient books. She is a writer and managing editor for The Cultivating Project, a contributing writer for The Rabbit Room, and co-director of the Anselm Arts Guild. Much of Amy's writing stems from wonder at the redemptive love of Christ and the piercing, reorienting grace of His joy. Ever seeking to "press on to [her] true country and to help others to do the same" (C. S. Lewis), she posts essays and stories about living Homeward at amybaiklee.com. She lives in Colorado with her husband and two daughters.

Junius Johnson

Junius Johnson is an independent scholar, musician, and writer with expertise in historical and systematic theology. He writes articles both scholarly and popular, considering theological aspects of beauty, imagination, and culture, and their implications for the Christian life. He holds a PhD in Philosophical Theology from Yale University and is the author of four books, including *The Father of Lights: A Theology of Beauty* (Baker Academic, 2020). An engaging speaker and teacher, he is a member of The Cultivating Project and offers online courses in theology, literature, and Latin through Junius Johnson Academics (academics.juniusjohnson.com).

Rex Bradshaw

Rex Bradshaw lives with his wife and daughter in Mississippi, where he is a member of St. Stephen's Anglican Church. He teaches economics and geography at Jackson Academy. He is at work on several literary projects and writes occasional essays on theology and education.

Album Credits

Produced by Matthew Clark
Mixed by Chris Bethea
Mastering by Voyager (Joe Causey)

Instrumentalists

Drums: Evan Walley (all tracks)
Bass: Itaiguara Brandão* (all tracks)
Synths: Evan Walley (2, 4, 7, 8, 10)
Additional keys and synth: Yifei Tang and Jonny Dyas** (4)
B3 organ: James Graham (1)
B3 organ and piano: Tyler Kemp (1, 5, 11)
Strings: Alon Hillel** (2, 6, 11)
Uilleann pipes and various Celtic goodies: Faliq Auri** (3, 9)
Pedal steel: Diederik van den Brandt** (7, 10)
Trumpet and sax: Dima Faustov** (2, 8)
Sarangi: Mayank Rathore (4)
Remaining vocals and instrumentation: Matthew Clark

*via Musiversal
**via Fiverr

CONNECT with MATTHEW

Sign up for Matthew Clark's newsletter and receive the latest updates on his music, writing, and podcast at

MATTHEWCLARK.NET

---

f @MATTHEWCLARKMUSIC   **◉** @MATTHEWCLARKNET

Did you enjoy this book?
If the answer is "yes," please share it with others!

- Share or mention *Only the Lover Sings* on your social media. Use the tags #TheWellTrilogy and #OnlytheLoverSingsAlbum to spread the word!

- Write a book review on your blog or on Amazon.

- Like the album and follow Matthew Clark on Spotify.

- Post this message on Twitter, Facebook, or Instagram: **I loved #OnlytheLoverSingsAlbum by @matthewclarknet!**

- Recommend this book for a Bible study or a book club.

- Share a copy with your friends and family.

- Follow Matthew Clark on Facebook, Instagram, YouTube, iTunes, and Spotify!